Library of
Davidson College

Selected Criticism and Parody of the Period

*A thirty-nine-volume facsimile set
essential to the study of one of the most
prolific periods in English literature*

*Edited by
William E. Fredeman, Ira Bruce Nadel, John F. Stasny*

A Garland Series

The Fleshly School of Poetry
Robert Buchanan

Under the Microscope
Algernon Charles Swinburne

Garland Publishing, Inc.
New York & London
1986

For a complete list of the titles in this series
see the final pages of this volume.

These facsimiles have been made from copies in
the Library of Congress.

Library of Congress Cataloging-in-Publication Data

Buchanan, Robert Williams, 1841–1901.
The fleshly school of poetry.

(The Victorian muse)
Reprint (1st work). Originally published: London :
Strahan, 1872.
Reprint (2nd work). Originally published: London :
D. White, 1872.
1. English poetry—19th century—History and
criticism.   I. Swinburne, Algernon Charles, 1837–1909.
Under the microscope. 1986. II. Title. III. Title:
Under the microscope. IV. Series.
PR594.B8   1986   821'.8'09   86-4801
ISBN 0-8240-8625-2 (alk. paper)

Design by Bonnie Goldsmith

The volumes in this series are printed on
acid-free, 250-year-life paper.

Printed in the United States of America

THE FLESHLY SCHOOL OF POETRY

AND OTHER PHENOMENA OF THE DAY

By ROBERT BUCHANAN

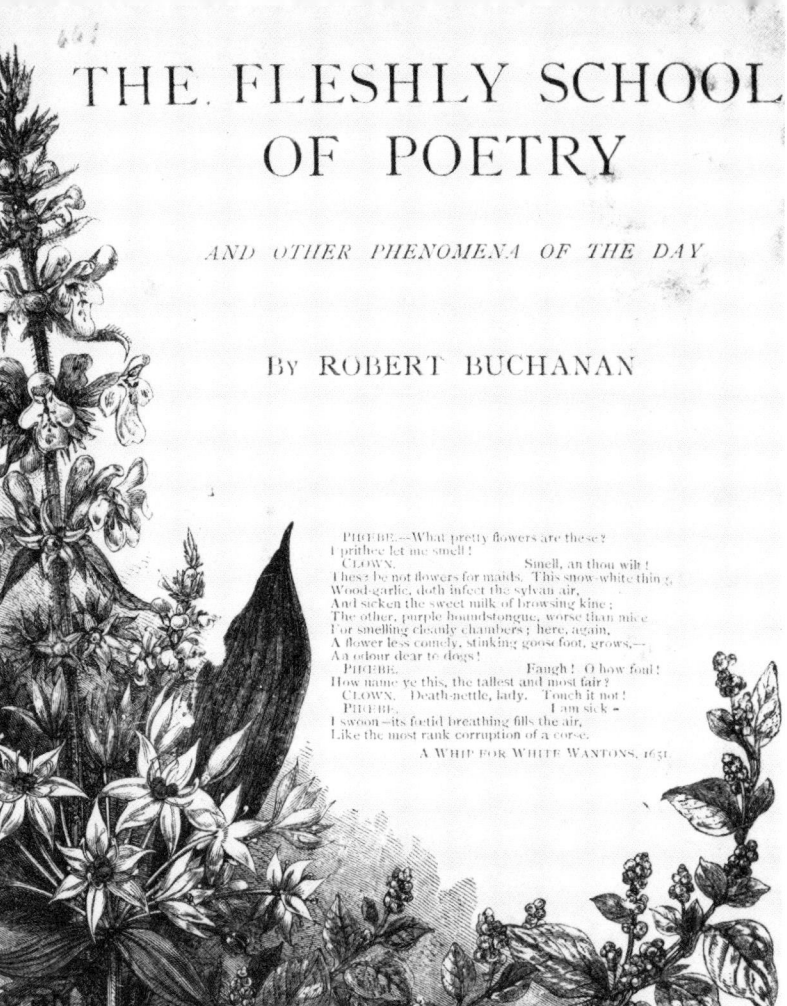

> PHŒBE.—What pretty flowers are these?
> I prithee let me smell!
> CLOWN.   Smell, an thou wilt!
> These be not flowers for maids. This snow-white thing,
> Wood-garlic, doth infect the sylvan air,
> And sicken the sweet milk of browsing kine;
> The other, purple houndstongue, worse than mice
> For smelling cleanly chambers; here, again,
> A flower less comely, stinking goose-foot, grows,—
> An odour dear to dogs!
> PHŒBE.   Faugh! O how foul!
> How name ye this, the tallest and most fair?
> CLOWN. Death-nettle, lady. Touch it not!
> PHŒBE.   I am sick—
> I swoon—its fœtid breathing fills the air,
> Like the most rank corruption of a corse.
>
> A WHIP FOR WHITE WANTONS, 1651.

STRAHAN & CO., 56, LUDGATE HILL, LONDON.

THE FLESHLY SCHOOL OF POETRY

AND OTHER PHENOMENA OF THE DAY

By ROBERT BUCHANAN

"For shame!—write cleanly, Labeo, or write none."
  HALL's *Satires*, Book II. 1.

"Belial came last, than whom a spirit more lewd
 Fell not from heaven, or more gross to love
 Vice for itself." *Paradise Lost.*

STRAHAN & CO., PUBLISHERS
56 LUDGATE HILL, LONDON
1872

LONDON:
PRINTED BY VIRTUE AND CO.,
CITY ROAD.

CONTENTS.

	PAGE
PREFACE	V

THE FLESHLY SCHOOL OF POETRY:

    I. SOCIAL PHENOMENA OF THE HOUR 1

    II. A LITERARY RETROSPECT: THE ITALIAN FALSETTO SINGERS AND THEIR IMITATORS 8

    III. CHARLES BAUDELAIRE AND A. C. SWINBURNE . . 16

    IV. MR. DANTE GABRIEL ROSSETTI 33

    V. THE "HOUSE OF LIFE," &C., RE-EXAMINED . . 56

    VI. PEARLS FROM THE AMATORY POETS 69

    VII. PROSPECTS OF THE FINAL DEGRADATION OF VERSE, AS A MEANS OF INTELLIGENT EXPRESSION . . 82

NOTES 92

PREFACE.

THE nucleus of the following Essay was published last October in the *Contemporary Review*, with the signature "Thomas Maitland" affixed to it (without my knowledge), *in order that the criticism might rest upon its own merits, and gain nothing from the name of the real writer.* At the time of the publication I myself was yachting among the Scottish Hebrides. As the obscure "Thomas Maitland," however, happened to have uttered an unpleasant and startling truth, the fleshly gentlemen moved heaven, earth, and Jupiter Pluvius in order to create a storm, and (carefully eschewing the real literary question) they have used all the means in their hands to demonstrate that the criticism was the malicious and cowardly work of a rival poet, afraid to strike in broad day or under his real name, and adopting a pseudonym to conceal his real identity. For the correspondence on this subject—for Mr. Rossetti's own defence and the opinion of Mr. Rossetti's friends, as well as for my own simple explanation of the facts of the case—the reader is referred to the *Athenæum* newspaper for December 16th and December 30th, 1871.

I have only one word to use concerning the attacks upon myself. They are the inventions of cowards, too spoilt with flattery to bear criticism, and too querulous and humorsome to perceive the real issues of the case.

My imputed crime is as follows: that I did not sign my own name to the article, and that I spoke in high terms of my own poems.

The first account has been disposed of by the simple statement that I did not sign the article at all. If it be retorted that the rule of the *Contemporary Review* is never to admit pseudonyms or unsigned articles, I answer that at least three of the regular contributors to that *Review* have habitually used pseudonyms, and that, in an early number of the same publication, Dean Mansell sharply criticized Mr. Mill in an unsigned article in which he spoke of himself in the third person, afterwards reprinting the article, with his own name, as "The Philosophy of the Conditioned."

The second count, which charges me with secret self-praise, is so absurd an attempt to distract judgment that it is almost unworthy of mention. In an opening paragraph (now suppressed for its weakness) I drew out a sort of sketch of *Hamlet* as "cast" by ¡the contemporary poets, Mr. Tennyson of course assuming the leading character; and among the list of smaller parts I humorously spoke of myself as playing the part of—what? Horatio? The King? Polonius? Rosencranz? Guildenstern? Osric? Of none of these, small or great, but simply that of "Cornelius!" I imagined then that I was writing for readers who had read their Shakspere, or who had at any rate seen his great tragedy murdered on the stage, and never dreamt I should have to explain (as I am now forced to explain) that "Cornelius" is one of those two gentlemen who appear in Scene II. in the usual way of what are technically known as "utility" people, and after uttering together this one memorable line—

"In this and all things will we show our duty!"—

exeunt in all humility. In a subsequent scene they return, and Voltimand, the *other* gentleman, makes a speech, while "Cornelius" stands in the usual "utility" attitude, with one leg bent and one hand laid gracefully on his hips. This is the proud character I am accused of arrogating to myself in the grand list of contemporary performances! Surely, if I had been ambitious of obtruding my own merits, I might at least have gone in for Fortinbras or the First Gravedigger!

The other allusion to "my own poems" will be found on page 46 of this pamphlet. It simply chronicles a fact, and is neither complimentary nor the reverse.

The truth is, all this hubbub about the authorship is a vulgar farce, got up to distract public attention. My article was altered and my name suppressed with the best of all motives—that of letting the charges contained in it stand on their own merits, and that of saving me from the persecution of a clique of literary Mohawks; but it is a pity any alteration was made at all.

Be that as it may, let me entreat my readers not to let their attention be distracted by any consideration of me personally. Let them carefully accept and weigh the evidence brought forward in these pages, and judge the case on its own merits. The clatter that is being made about the authorship is only meant to excite the public against a patient examination of this "most damning" indictment against the Fleshly School of Poetry.

The most curious part of the whole affair remains to be

told. It is delightful as showing the ratio of public intelligence. It appears that these poems of Mr. Rossetti have actually become favourites with that prude of prudes, the British matron; and several gentlemen tell me that their aunts and grandmothers see no harm in them! My own grandmother is not poetical, so I have not sought her opinion. But here I am front to front with the amazing fact that a large section of cultured people read poetry, and enjoy it, without the faintest perception of what it is all about—without the slightest wish to realise the images or the situations—without any more intellectual effort than they use when having their hair brushed! Conceive the mental state of the aunt or grandmother who could read such verses as this—

> "I was a child beneath her touch—a man
> When *breast to breast we clung*, even I and she,
> A spirit when her spirit looked thro' me,—
> A god when *all our life-breath met to fan
> Our life's-blood, till love's emulous ardours ran,
> Fire within fire, desire in deity!*"—

and merely think them sweetly pretty. It is hard to think ill of one's relations; but the mature females in question must be either very obtuse, or—very, very naughty!

The truth appears to be, that writing, however nasty, will be perfectly sanctified to English readers if it be moral in the legal sense; and thus a poet who describes sensual details may do so with impunity if he labels his poems—"Take notice! These sensations are strictly *nuptial;* these delights have been sanctioned by English law, and registered at Doctors' Commons!" We have here the reason that Mr. Rossetti has almost escaped censure, while Mr. Swinburne has been punished so severely; for Mr. Rossetti, in his worst poems, explains that he is speaking dramatically in the character of a *husband* addressing his *wife*. Animalism is animalism, nevertheless, whether licensed or not; and, indeed, one might tolerate the language of lust more readily on the lips of a lover addressing a mistress than on the lips of a husband virtually (in these so-called "Nuptial" Sonnets) wheeling his nuptial couch out into the public streets.

ROBERT BUCHANAN.

I.

"Shakspere's an infernal humbug, Pip! I never read him. What the devil is it all about, Pip? There's a lot of feet in Shakspere's verse, but there ain't any legs worth mentioning in Shakspere's plays, are there, Pip? .... Let us have plenty of leg pieces, Pip, and I'll stand by you!"—DICKENS'S *Martin Chuzzlewit*.

THOUGH this is a generation of great poets and teachers; though Tennyson, Browning, Victor Hugo, Carlyle, Emerson, and Walt Whitman are still amongst us, while Dickens (essentially a poet) and Landor have not long left us; though much of our public teaching (and notably that of the public press) is lofty and clean, there are not wanting signs that Sensualism, which from time immemorial has been the cancer of all society, is shooting its ulcerous roots deeper and deeper, and blotching more and more the fair surface of things. Coming this winter from a remote retreat in the Highlands to this great centre of life which men have named London, moving from street to street and from house to house, seeing all that a man with eyes can see, what are the objects which most impress themselves upon me? Not the old immemorial squalor of the slums, the hideous famine of the by-streets and lanes, the gaudy misery in numberless human faces (that is no novelty); nor the fatuous imbecility and superficiality of the moneyed vulgar, and the shapeless ugliness of women who feed high and take no exercise (that, too, is familiar, though not perhaps on so large a scale); nor the dark blotches of life where disease squats for ever, nor the follies of the last new fashion, nor the hideousness of the last new public building. All these things are passed on one side, as I approach a phenomenon so strange and striking that to a superstitious mind it might seem a portent, and so hideous that it converts this great city of civilisation into a great Sodom or Gomorrah waiting for doom. Look which way I will, the horrid thing threatens and paralyzes me. It lies on the drawing-room table, shamelessly naked and dangerously fair. It is part of the pretty poem which the belle of the season reads, and it breathes away the pureness of her soul like the poisoned breath of the girl in Hawthorne's tale. It covers the shelves of the great Oxford-Street librarian, lurking in the covers of three-volume novels. It is on the French booksellers' counters, authenticated by the signature of the author of the " Visite de Noces." It is here, there, and everywhere, in art, literature, life, just as surely as it is in the " Fleurs de Mal," the Marquis de Sade's " Justine," or the " Monk " of Lewis. It appeals to all tastes, to all dispositions, to all ages. If the querulous man of letters has his " Baudelaire," the pimpled clerk has his *Day's Doings*,* and the dissipated artisan his

---

* Publications of this sort are at last being taken seriously in hand by the Society for the Suppression of Vice. As I write, the following appears in the weekly journals:—"THE 'DAY'S DOINGS' AGAIN.— At Bow-street police-court on Thursday, Frederick Shove, the publisher of the *Day's Doings*, an illustrated paper, appeared to a fresh summons, granted by Sir Thomas Henry, charged with publishing indecent prints and printed matter. Mr. Besley (instructed by Mr. Collette, of the Society for the Suppression of Vice) prosecuted; Mr. Laxton, as before,

Day and Night. The streets are full of it. Photographs of nude, indecent, and hideous harlots, in every possible attitude that vice can devise, flaunt from the shop-windows, gloated over by the fatuous glint of the libertine and the greedy open-mouthed stare of the day-labourer. Never was this Snake, which not all the naturalists of the world have been able to scotch, so vital and poisonous as now. It has penetrated into the very sweetshops; and there, among the commoner sorts of confectionery, may be seen this year models of the female Leg, the whole definite and elegant article as far as the thigh, with a fringe of paper cut in imitation of the female drawers and embroidered in the female fashion!

When things have come to such a pass as this, it is difficult to be quite serious in dealing with them. The foot-and-mouth disease is dreadful, but the Leg-disease, though generally fatal, is egregiously absurd into the bargain. Now, to begin with, there is nothing indecent in the human Leg itself; on the contrary, it is a most beautiful and useful member. Nor is it necessarily indecent to show the

---

defended. Mr. Besley said that a promise was made when the defendant was last summoned at this court that all matter or prints suggestive of indecency should be withdrawn for the future. He produced five copies of the *Day's Doings*, from which he read different articles of an obscene and vulgar nature, and pointed out a print of a nude woman, which was, in his opinion, even more objectionable. Mr. Laxton contended that the nude figure referred to was a copy of the work of a well-known artist, and to decrease its nudity drapery had been added to the figure. Sir Thomas Henry said the drapery was suggestive of even greater indecency. Sir Thomas Henry decided upon committing the case for trial, but said he would accept bail for the appearance of the defendant at the sessions, two sureties in £80 each, and the defendant's recognizances in £150."

Leg, as some ladies do upon the stage, without in the least shocking our propriety. But the Leg, an excellent thing in itself, becomes insufferable if obtruded into every concern of life, so that instead of humanity we see a demon resembling the Manx coat-of-arms, cutting capers without a body or a head. The Leg, as a disease, is subtle, secret, diabolical. It relies not merely on its own intrinsic attractions, but on its atrocious suggestions. It becomes a spectre, a portent, a mania. Turn your eyes to the English stage. Shakspere is demolished and lies buried under hecatombs of Leg! Open the last new poem. Its title will possibly be this, or similar to this—"Leg is enough." Walk along the streets. The shop-windows teem with Leg. Enter a music-hall—Leg again, and (O tempora! O mores!) the Can-Can. Jack enjoys it down Wapping way just as Jones does in the Canterbury Hall. It is only in fashionable rooms and in the stalls of the theatre that Leg is at a discount; but that is not because life there is more innocent and modest, but because Leg is in the higher circles altogether eclipsed by its two most formidable rivals—Bosom and Back.

If popular writers are to be credited, there is running rampant in English society a certain atrocious form of vice, a monster with two heads—one of which is called Adultery, the other Dipsomania—and these two heads, blind to all else in the world, leer and ogle at each other. I have not sufficient knowledge of English polite society to say whether or not the terrible impeachment is based on a careful study of facts; but I do know that the writings in which these facts have been chronicled, the prurient pictures given of vice masking in the garb of virtue, become in their turn, and for the very sake of the imputations they contain, the delight of vulgar débauchés and heartless libertines. No form of animal is more common than he who, when charged with folly and immorality, retorts with a smile—" All very well, but I am no worse than my neighbours; virtue—fudge! there is no such thing, at least in English society; everything is bought and sold;"—and this enlightened person, hearing on the best authority that love of the best sort procurable and lust of the gaudiest sort possible are equally in the market for the highest bidder, prefers purchasing his indulgence as the humour seizes him to making a bargain for a life-luxury of which he may get thoroughly tired. Nothing, meantime, gratifies the free lover more than to be told that marriage is a farce and continence a sham, that all forms of life are equally heartless, and that his betters in the social scale only commit in secret the follies in which he indulges openly. Is it true, then, that English society is honeycombed and rotten? More than one form of literature says so. The smart journal says so. So does the novel of the period. So does the artistic Bohemian. For my own part I am inclined to believe (though, as I have said, on very insufficient knowledge) that true English life is infinitely purer and better than our smart writers and lady novelists imagine it to be; that the pure rose of English maidenhood still blows as brightly as ever; that, in a word, the canker lies on the surface and has not *yet* eaten down into the body social. How then account for the portentous symptoms which are everywhere appalling us? Thus. There is on the fringe of real English society, and chiefly, if not altogether, in London here, a sort of demi-monde, not composed, like that other in France, of simple courtesans, but of men and women of indolent habits and æsthetic tastes, artists, literary persons, novel writers, actors, men of genius and men of talent, butterflies and gadflies of the human kind, leading a lazy existence from hand to mouth. These persons "write for the papers." They publish books, often at their own expense. They, some of them, have titles. They belong to clubs and they go to dinner parties. They paint pictures, sometimes good ones. They compose music, generally bad music. They lecture on art and literature to young ladies' schools. They read Balzac, Dumas *fils*, and the "cerebellic" autobiographies of Goethe. They are clever, refined, interesting, able, querulous. Nothing delights them more than to tear a reputation to pieces or to diagnose the seeds of moral disease in the healthiest subjects. Their religion is called culture, their narrow-mindedness is called insight. Their portraits are sold, along with those of nude harlots and lascivious courtesans, at a shilling per head in the public streets. Two peculiarities distinguish this class of persons to a careful eye—they are as oblivious to the fact that life has a past as that the soul has a future, and they are never by any chance seen in that English society which they profess to understand so thoroughly.

Now, if we carefully consider the question we are discussing, we shall in all possibility find that all the gross and vulgar conceptions of life which are formulated into certain products of art, literature, and criticism, emanate from this Bohemian class. Its members do not, we believe, penetrate far into life of any kind, but where they do penetrate they create the vices they perceive, and reflect phenomena in the distorted mirrors of their own moral consciousness. Possessing no religion, they imagine that English life is irreligious. Having no faith, they perceive no faith anywhere. Ingenious almost to diablerie, they will prove to you by critical theory that art is simply the method of getting most sweets out of one's living sensations—the knack, to put it metaphorically, of sucking your lollipop so as to extract out of it the best possible flavour. If a man speaks to them earnestly, they will smile and style him "didactic." If a man writes for them religiously, they will inwardly congratulate themselves on having passed quite beyond "that sort of thing." These men—and alas! these women—compose some of our poetry, paint some of our pictures, write a good deal of our formal criticism. Is it any wonder, therefore, that the poor bewildered public shakes its head over the terrible accounts put before it, and begins slowly but surely to share the scepticism and flippancy it at first considered so shocking? Is it any wonder that Leg-literature flourishes? Is it any wonder that wise men like Mr. Ruskin rail, and philosophers like Mr. Carlyle despair? There lies the seat of the cancer—there, in the Bohemian fringe of society. Will no courageous hand essay to cut it out? Will no physician come to put his finger in the true seat of the sore? There it is, spreading daily like all cancerous diseases, foul in itself and creating foulness. If we cannot destroy it altogether with some terrible caustic, let us at least take precautions to prevent it from spreading. The disease is worth the remedy, the remedy is worth a prayer.

It is my business in the present pages to deal only with one form of the moral phenomenon, to regard Sensualism only in so far as it affects contemporary poetry. My plan was at first broader, but I find it beyond my present materials. To deal with the question completely, to pass in review the effects of Sensualism on art, on music, on the drama, and above all to trace its physiological causes and consequences as expressed in all these different directions, would occupy far more time than I am able to bestow on the subject. Let me hope, however, that others may speak, now I have spoken, adding to mine their testimony and their protest.

II.

> " Whilom the sisters nine were vestal maids . . .
> But since, I saw it painted on Fame's wings,
> The Muses to be woxen wantonings.
> Ye bastard poets, see your progeny!"
> BISHOP HALL.

THE true history of European poetry is the history of European progress, from the narrow microscopic pedantry of mediæval culture to the large telescopic sweep of modern thought and science. It is no part of my present plan to attempt the historical subject, except in so far as it affects the phenomena of the present day; and I need only indicate, therefore, how the ever-broadening poetry of humanity has flowed to us in one varying stream of increase since the day when, as Denham sings—

> "Old Chaucer, like the morning star,
> To us discovered day from far."

Chaucer and his contemporaries were, as all readers know, under deep obligations to the poets and romancists of mediæval Italy; and it is a most significant token of Chaucer's pre-eminent originality that, while Gower and the rest had only been inspired to imitate what was bad in the great models, he, on the contrary, merely derived inspiration and solace from their music, assimilated what was noble in it, and carefully prepared a breezier and healthier poetic form of his own. What is grandest and best in Chaucer is Chaucer's exclusively. No better proof can be had of his merit as the morning star of the modern school than a careful comparison of him, first with Boccaccio, then with Dante. All the limpid flow of narrative, the concentration and pomp of subject, all the lighter humour and sparkle, are to be found in the "Decameron." All the dramatic intensity, the quaint but tender realism, are (with mighty qualities superadded) to be discovered in Dante. But the quaint saline humour, the universality of sympathy, the childlike love of nature, and the supreme piteousness of modern poetry, dawned with the divine author of the "Canterbury Tales." Chaucer was emphatically the poet of the bourgeoisie, just as Shakspere and his brethren were the poets of the feudal idea; but with all these writers alike, with the author of the "Wife of Bath" as well as with the creator of Falstaff, humanity was beginning to get such a hearing for itself, and notably on the humorous side of the question, as would be certain in the long-run to blend both ideas, that of feudalism and that of the bourgeoisie, into the great modern sentiment of popular rights, duties, and affections. The great dramatists of the reign of Elizabeth, following in Chaucer's footsteps, appear, under some awful demoniac influence (for individually these men were destitute of beneficence), to have prepared for modern contemplation an unequalled gallery of human faces and souls—a gallery all-embracing in its range, photographing the meanest as well as the highest, and revealing to us, under all the dazzle and glitter of a sumptuous feudal style, the instincts which all men have in common, the compensations which each owes to the other, and the fair world in which each has an equal and indisputable share. Simply to picture men "in their habits as they live," no matter under what motive, was the highest possible beneficence; and this, in the golden dawn of our poetry, was done inimitably, with a beauty of thought and a wealth of resource unknown to any poet that has appeared since.

Such was the dawn of our poetry; and did ever dawn bid promise of a more glorious day?

But, alas! to the reddening of this fair promise succeeded no fulfilment. Just when light seemed fullest, time and season were miraculously altered, and a period arrived, an overclouding of the sun, a portentous darkness, wherein few could tell whether it was night or day. This darkness was of a vaporous nature, miasmic. It was a fever-cloud generated first in Italy and then blown westward; finally, after sucking up all that was most unwholesome from the soil of France, to fix itself on England, and breed in its direful shadow a race of monsters whose long line has not ceased from that to the present day.

Just previously to and contemporaneously with the rise of Dante, there had flourished a legion of poets of greater or less ability, but all more or less characterized by affectation, foolishness, and moral blindness: singers of the falsetto school, with ballads to their mistress's eyebrow, sonnets to their lady's lute, and general songs of a fiddlestick; peevish men for the most part, as is the way of all fleshly and affected beings ; men so ignorant of human subjects and materials as to be driven, in their sheer bankruptcy of mind, to raise Hope, Love, Fear, Rage (everything but Charity) into human entities, and to treat the body and upholstery of a dollish woman as if, in itself, it constituted a whole Universe. In the ways of these poor devils Dante walked a little ; and he has left us, in his "Vita Nuova," a book which carries the system of individual fantasy about as near perfection as possible, and (of course) invests a radically absurd line of thought with a fictitious and tremendous interest. The "Vita Nuova" is enormously fine in its way, as the self-revelation of a man in whom the world is interested, and to whom many conceits may be freely pardoned. It is quaint, fine, subtle, suggestive ; but its chief value is this, that it was composed, in a tender moment, by the tremendous creature who wrote the story of Roman Catholicism in unfaltering and colossal cipher for the study of all forthcoming ages.

What was great and potent in Dante remained in the "Divine Comedy" and bore no seed. What was absurd and unnatural in Dante, mingling with foul exhalations from the brains of his brother poets, formed the miasmic cloud which obscured all English culture, generated madness even as far north as Hawthornden and Edinburgh, obscured Chaucer for centuries, darkened the way to the vast spaces of the Elizabethan drama, and generally bred in the very bones and marrow of English literature the veriest ague of absurdity ever known to keep human creature crazy. Surrey, a naturally strong man, sickened and died in the fever ; his limpid English just preserving his foolish subjects from total oblivion ; while Wyatt, affected in form as well as in substance, lingered through a long life of literary disease. Spenser and Drayton caught the complaint early, but, being men of robust genius, survived it. Shakspere had it, but his mighty spirit almost beautified disease itself, till he cast it off altogether, and clomb to the heaven-kissing hill where he wrote his plays. Poor old John Donne had the strangest possible attacks; he made a hard fight to recover his natural English health, but the reiterated relapses were too much for him; and there he lies, with his books on his breast, quaint as a carven figure on a tomb—and as unreal. How name over all the other victims who died literary death in those days? How call up before the reader the sad shades of Davies, Carew, William Drummond, the two Fletchers, Habington, and all those once famous British bards? Gliding onward through the spectral host, we pass Crashaw, a Rossetti of the period, with twice the genius and half the advantages; and Suckling, immortal by virtue of his one true note—the "Ballad on a Wedding;" and Browne, the Elizabethan Keats, with his falsetto voice and occasional tones of really delicious cunning; till latterly, in a languid and depressed state of mind, we arrive before the prone figure of Cowley, who essayed to drive the very horses of the sun, and came to the cruel earth with a smash so prodigious. Poor ghosts! To think of it! All these persons were admired in their generation. Frankincense of praise and myrrh of flattery had been theirs to the full. They flattered each other, and they tickled the age. What pleased the public mind in Shakspere was the "quaint conceits" of his "wonderful" sonnets; his plays were nowhere for the time being. The Italian disease raged and devastated art, literature, and society. Now it was the simple sentimental form, light and dainty, symptomised by such verses as "To Roses in the Bosom of Castara," "Upon Cupid's Death and Burial in Cynthia's Cheeke," or "On a Mole in Celia's Bosom." Again it was the dull metaphysical type, deep-seated and incurable, with its "Negative Love," its "Answer to the Platonics," and "Love's Visibility." At one time the disease was scrofulous and foul-mouthed, sending forth addresses "To His Mistress's going to Bed," and "On the Happiness of a Flea on Celia's Body." At another the religious mania supervened, and all the language of passion was applied to divine things, startling us with coquettish addresses to the Magdalen, to "Mary's Tear," "On the Blessed Virgin's Bashfulness," and so on. But in all these cases, however extraordinary, however fatal, two results could be noted. The performances of the diseased persons afforded intense delight to a certain section of the public, and the amount of contemporary eulogy was almost always in proportion to the fatal nature of the disease.

With Cowley, the epidemic seemed to culminate. This prodigy of success overdid his character, and it seemed impossible for the lover's vein to be carried further by any other ambitious Bottom. Milton corrected his system with the strong tonics of the ancients; and Dryden, when he rose, fortified himself with the disinfectant of Roman satire. Nevertheless the disease lingered in the land, co-operating with new diseases from the corrupt court of France. It would be tiresome indeed to name all the poor creatures, from Cowley to Spratt, who suffered and died, more or less under the fatal influence. It was in positive despair, to resist the epidemic, that English literature hardened into the formal cleanliness of the Addisonian period. Classicism was used as an antidote, while Ambrose Phillips was delighting "society" with pieces like that "On the Little Lady Charlotte Pulteney drest to go to a Ball." * False love, false heroics, false pastoral pictures, false life, false thought, all more or less consequent on the foul corruptions from Italy and France, had shaken the whole fabric of English literature when Jonathan Swift composed his mock-erotic verses "On a beautiful Young Nymph going to Bed," and Pope & Co. their "Martinus Scriblerus on the Art of Sinking in Poetry;" but neither Pope nor Swift was strong enough to inaugurate a new and nobler art. English poetry was virtually dead.

A tranquil gleam of honest English light came with Cowper, whose patient and gentle services have scarcely yet been rated at their true worth. But the true seeds of a new life had been scattered abroad when Bishop Percy published his "Reliques." These seeds were slow to spring, the slower because they sank so deep. At last, however, Wordsworth came, and English literature was saved. Then, with one loud trumpet-note, Byron amazed matrons and disarmed critics. Then, with a shining face, Coleridge uttered stately syllables of mightiest thought. Then, too, Southey gave his help, now unjustly forgotten. Then Lamb and Hazlitt began to criticize, directing men's eyes back to the true fount of English thought and diction—the tales of Chaucer and the Elizabethan drama. Then Scott arose, simple and deep as the sea—freighted with golden argosies of history and lighted with the innumerable laughter of the waves.

* These verses are worth studying, as showing how the only effect produced on the "poet of the period" by the sight of a little female child was the regret that the infant was not yet old enough "to be made love to."

Then indeed poor England shook off her taint, and felt her heart beat with a truer, freer pulse,—

> "For a sweet wind from heaven had come
> To blow her cares away."

Hope had come at last—more than a gleam,—a glorious azure burst. It was sad to think how many centuries had been wasted; but the invalid-literature of this country was not quite dead.

Strange to say, just at that very moment, when things looked brightest, honest Gifford had to demolish the Della Cruscan school, and Canning and Frere found it necessary to destroy Dr. Darwin. In both of these maniacal manifestations, but particularly in the former, society and the small critics of the day delighted. The Della Cruscan poems were sung to guitars, and warbled by young ladies at their embroidery frames. They had one recommendation —they were harmless. They were neither demoralising nor dirty. They died a very speedy death, when once Gifford took the trouble to exterminate them; but perhaps they hardly needed so severe an operation. In our own day we have had, besides the Fleshly School under notice, the Spasmodic School, headed by Bailey, Smith, and Dobell; but these poets possessed great purity, and were unfairly treated. The worst argument against them was their comparative poetic silence after the date of Aytoun's attacks. All these so-called Schools over-exert themselves and end in phthisis. A great poet is a law to himself, and does not work in groups.

After this last futile development, the Italian disease would possibly have died out altogether. That it has not died, has been due to a fresh importation of the obnoxious matter from France. The Scrofulous School of Literature had been distinguishing itself for many a long year in Paris, but it reached its final and most tremendous development in Charles Baudelaire,—a writer to whom I must now direct the reader's attention.

III.

CHARLES BAUDELAIRE.

"Je cherche le vide, et le noir, et le nu!"
"I seek the Black, the Empty, and the Nude!"
Fleurs de Mal.

I HAVE before me, as I write, the portrait of Baudelaire, the memoir by Gautier, the original edition of the "Fleurs de Mal," and the collected edition of Baudelaire's works, published since his death.

Gautier's memoir is a miracle of cunning writing, containing hardly a syllable with which one disagrees, and yet skilfully and secretly poisoning the mind of any unsuspicious reader. The best antidote I can recommend against such clever trash is the tiniest pinch of humour, the least sense of the absurd; for directly the whole thing is put in the proper light, contempt yields to laughter, and laughter dies away in pity for the poor "æstheticized" figures to whom we are being introduced. It may also be as well, at the same time, to call to mind how even the mighty genius of George Sand, at first so promising and so commanding (in those days when even Mazzini's pure soul did it homage), slowly decomposed under the inner action of the artistic and self-critical instinct, until it falsified all hopes, and ended in utter demoralisation. This literary finessing, this intellectual fingering, constitutes a tithe of the genius of Hugo, a half of the genius of George Sand, the whole of the genius of Charles Baudelaire and his biographer. A little Shaksperian sense of quiddity would soon show us what a poor, attenuated, miserable scarecrow of humanity Baudelaire was in reality, and what a mere serving-man, self-deluded and self-deluding, is this poor old Gautier-Malvolio, who holds forth, "cross-garter'd," over his grave.

Gautier first met Baudelaire in "that grand salon in the most pure style of Louis XIV.," where the hasheesh-eaters of Paris were wont to hold their meetings; and his description of the furniture of this chamber is very great, quite in the spirit of a French upholsterer. Here is his vignette portrait of Baudelaire as he appeared on that occasion :—

"Son aspect nous frappa : il avait les cheveux coupés très ras et du plus beau noir ; ces cheveux, faisant des pointes régulières sur le front d'une éclatante blancheur, le coiffaient comme une espèce de casque sarrasin ; les yeux, couleur de tabac d'Espagne, avaient un regard spirituel, profond, et d'une pénétration peut-être un peu trop insistante ; quant à la bouche, meublée de dents très-blanches, elle abritait, sous une légère et soyeuse moustache ombrageant son contour, des sinuosités mobiles, voluptueuses et ironiques comme les lèvres des figures peintes par Léonard de Vinci ; le nez, fin et délicat, un peu arrondi, aux narines palpitantes, semblait subodorer de vagues parfums lointains ; une fossette vigoureuse accentuait le menton comme le coup de pouce final du statuaire ; les joues, soigneusement rasées, contrastaient, par leur fleur bleuâtre que veloutait la poudre de riz, avec les nuances vermeilles des pommettes ; le cou, d'une élégance et d'une blancheur féminines, apparaissait dégagé, partant d'un col de chemise rabattu et d'une étroite cravate en madras des Indes et à carreaux. Son vêtement consistait en un paletôt d'une étoffe noire lustrée et brillante, un pantalon noisette, des bas blancs et des escarpins vernis, le tout méticuleusement propre et correct, avec un cachet voulu de simplicité anglaise et comme l'intention de se séparer du genre artiste, à chapeaux de feutre mou, à vestes de velours, à vareuses rouges, à barbe prolixe et à crinière échevelée. Rien de trop frais ni de trop voyant dans cette tenue rigoureuse. Charles Baudelaire appartenait à ce dandysme sobre qui râpe ses habits avec du papier de verre pour leur ôter l'éclat endimanché et tout battant neuf si cher au philistin et si désagréable pour le vrai gentleman. Plus tard même, il rasa sa moustache, trouvant que c'était un reste de vieux chic pittoresque qu'il était puéril et bourgeois de conserver."—*Œuvres de Baudelaire, précédées d'une notice par Théophile Gautier, Paris,* 1869.

This interesting creature, with his nose sniffing "distant perfumes," his carefully-shaven cheeks, and his general air of man-millinery, was in earnest conversation with the "model" Maryx, who, with the immobility acquired in the studio, was reclining on a couch, resting her superb head on a cushion, and attired "in a white robe, quaintly starred with red spots resembling drops of blood!" Hard by, at the window, sat another superb female, known as "La Femme au Serpent," from having sat to Clevinger when he painted his picture of that name. The latter, having thrown on a fauteuil "her mantle of black lace and the most delicious little green hood that ever covered Lucy Hocquet or Madame Baudraud, shook her yellow lioness-locks, still humid, for she came from the swimming school (L'Ecole de Natation), and from all her body, clad in muslin, exhaled like a naiad the fresh perfume of the bath!" In the same company were Jean Fenchères, the sculptor, and Jean Boissard, the latter with "his red mouth, teeth of pearl, and brilliant complexion." One scarcely knows which to admire most in this description,—the writer's fine apotheosis of the *lupanar* into an "artistic decameron," or the avidity with which he seizes on personal traits and on male and female millinery. He is "up" in both under and over-clothing, as worn by both sexes. He is, moreover, candour itself. He makes no secret of Baudelaire's little weaknesses and his own. "With an air quite simple, natural, and perfectly disengaged, he advanced some axiom satanically monstrous, or sustained with an icy *sang-froid* some theory of a mathematical exactness; for there was a vigorous method in the development of his absurdities." In a word, it is not denied that Baudelaire was that most unsympathetic of all beings, a cold sensualist, and that he carried into all his pleasures (until they slew him) the dandyism and the self-possession of a true child of Mephistopheles.

After a youth spent in wanderings in the East, and in acquiring, as Gautier naïvely says, "that love of the black Venus, for whom he had always a taste," Baudelaire returned to Paris, rented a little *chambre de garçon*, and assumed all the privileges of a literary life in the most debauched city of the world. His reading, which seems to have been of a very limited nature, developed his already singular disposition into true literary monstrosity, and the morbid nature of his tastes may be gathered from the fact that his first public effort was a translation of the American Tales of Edgar Poe. To Poe he seems to have borne an extraordinary resemblance, both in genius and in character. Equally clever, affected, and cold-blooded; equally incredulous of goodness and angry at philanthropy; equally self-indulgent and sensual, he lived as useless a life, died as wretched a death, and left for his legacy books even more worthless — the very dregs of his unhappy and sunless moral nature. Like Poe and Swinburne, he affected innovations in verse, and sought out the most morbid themes for poetical treatment. Encouraged by Poe, he tried to surpass him on his own ground—to triumph over him in the diablerie of horror. Encouraged in his turn, Mr. Swinburne has attempted to surpass Baudelaire, and to excel even that frightful artist in the representation of abnormal types of diseased lust and lustful disease.

"Art," said Baudelaire in effect, "has but one object, like life—that of exciting in the reader's soul the sensation of enjoyment. What poetry is to life, the drug hasheesh is to me personally, enabling me to extract supreme enjoyment out of the sheerly diabolical ideas of my own mind. I despise humanity, and I approve the devil." Animated by these noble sentiments, he killed himself by self-indulgence, and virtually exclaimed to the youth of France, with his dying breath, "Go ye and do likewise!"

I know well how much may be said in defence of a man like this by a wise and beneficent criticism; but I know, too, that defence has been overwrought, till mercy for the sinner has enlarged into sympathy with the sin. I am well aware, moreover—no man can be better aware—of the *charm* of writers like Baudelaire, and even of a certain service they may do to literature by careful attention to æsthetic form. Having few ideas, they endeavour to express them neatly, and with novelty. But no good can come to life or literature from the atrocious system of painting such figures in the light voluptuous colours of art; of exalting such contemptible persons into first-rate literary positions, and of evading the moral of their lives for the sake of pointing an epigram and delighting the fool. Charles Baudelaire lived and died a slave to his own devil; every line he wrote was slave's work; every picture he ever painted was in one hue—the dark blood-tint of his own shame. And yet it is this man, this dandy of the brothel, this Brummel of the stews, this fifth-rate *littérateur*, who, adopting to a certain extent the self-explanatory and querulous system of the Italian school of poets, and carefully avoiding the higher issues of that noble school of which Hugo is the living head, has been chosen (by no angel certainly) to be the godfather as it were of the modern Fleshly School, and thus to fill the select salon of English literature with a perfume to which the smell of Mrs. Aphra Behn's books is savoury, and that of Catullus' "lepidum novum libellum" absolutely delicious.

This is our double misfortune—to have a nuisance, and to have it at second hand. We might have been more tolerant to an unclean thing, if it had been in some sense a product of the soil. We have never been foolish purists, here in England. We freely forgave Byron many a wicked turn, because we knew he loved much, because we saw how much he was the product of national forces darkly working to the light. We welcomed Goethe, even when he sent the "Elective Affinities" and the cerebellic autobiographies. But to be overrun with the brood of an inferior French sonnetteer, whose only originality was his hideousness of subject, whose only merit was in his nasal appreciation of foul odours, surely that is far too much: it would have been a little too much twenty years ago, when the Empire began creating its viper's nest in the heart of France; it is a hundred times too much *now*, when the unclean place has been burnt with avenging fire.

A few years before his death, Baudelaire published hi chief work—" Fleurs de Mal." This book was a little too strong even for Paris under the Empire; so the censor came down, and some of the vilest poems were ruthlessly expunged. But Baudelaire gained his end, and secured a spurious notoriety. Some years later Mr. Swinburne thought the French poet's success worthy of emulation, and he therefore published his "Poems and Ballads," which was so very hot that his publishers dropped it like a blazing cinder in the very month of publication, and only one publisher, who shall be nameless, had the courage to lift it up.

All that is worst in Mr. Swinburne belongs to Baudelaire. The offensive choice of subject, the obtrusion of unnatural passion, the blasphemy, the wretched animalism, are all taken intact out of the "Fleurs de Mal." Pitiful! that any sane man, least of all any English poet, should think this dunghill worthy of importation! In the centre of his collection Baudelaire placed the most horrid poem ever written by man, a poem unmatched for simple hideousness even in Rome during the decadence—a piece worthy to be spoken by Ascyltos in Petronius Arbiter—and entitled "Femmes Damnées." The interlocutors in this piece are two women, who have just been guilty of the vilest act conceivable in human debauchery, but the theme and the treatment are too loathsome for description. Encouraged by the hideousness of "Femmes Damnées," Mr. Swinburne attempted to beat it in "Anactoria," a poem the subject of which is again that branch of crime which is generally known as the Sapphic passion. It would be tedious, apart from the unsavouriness of the subject, to pursue the analogy much further through individual poems. Perhaps the best plan is to give a few specimens of Baudelaire's quality, and leave the reader to compare them with Mr. Swinburne's book at leisure.

In the very first poem of his collection Baudelaire avows

his true character, and accuses the reader of being not a whit better :—

> "Hypocrite lecteur,—mon semblable,—mon frère!"

He purposes, he says, on his way (the way of all humanity) down to absolute Hell, to pass in review a few of the horrors he sees on his path. His way lies—

> "Parmi les chacals, les panthères, les lices,
> Les singes, les scorpions, les vautours, les serpents,
> *Les monstres glapissants, hurlants, grognants, rampants
> Dans la ménagerie infâme de nos vices!*"

And of all these monsters the most infernal is—L'Ennui! The very next poem sweetly chronicles the birth of the Poet, whose mother, affrighted and blaspheming, stretches her hands to God, crying : " Cursed be that night of fleeting pleasure, when my womb conceived my punishment !" In the next poem the poet is compared to the albatross, splendid on the wing, but almost unable to walk ; and the comparison strikes me as very applicable to this poet himself, only that his whole book is a waddling, unwieldy, and unsuccessful attempt to begin a flight. In a number of short lyrics he talks of poetry, music, and life, without affording us much edification (save in a really powerful picture called " Don Juan in Hell") till he begins to sing, not the delights of the flesh, but the morbid feelings of satiety. Accustomed to the Swinburnian female, we at once recognise her here in the original, as the serpent that dances, the cat that scratches and cries, and the large-limbed sterile creature who never conceives. She " bites," of course :—

> "Pour exercer les dents à ce jeu singulier,
> Il se faut chaque jour un cœur au râtelier!"

She has "cold eyelids that shut like a jewel:"—

> "Tes yeux, où rien ne se révèle
> De doux ni d'amer,
> Sont *deux bijoux froids !*"

She is cold and "sterile:"—

> "La froide majesté de la femme stérile !"

She is, necessarily, like "a snake:"—

> ... "un serpent qui danse," &c., &c.

She is, in fact, Faustine, Mary Stuart, Our Lady of Pain, Sappho, and all the rest,—quite as nasty, and to all intents and purposes, in spite of her attraction for young poets, seemingly as undesirable.

It is quite impossible for me, without long quotation, to fully represent the unpleasantness of Baudelaire, with his "vampires," his "cats," and "cat-like women," his poisons, his fiends, his phantoms, his long menagerie of horrors, his long catalogue of debaucheries. At one time we are in a brothel, and the poet is lying by the side of a dreadful Jewess with "cold eyelids:"—

> "Une nuit que j'étais près d'une affreuse Juive,
> *Comme au long d'un cadavre un cadavre étendu !*"

At another time we hear the poet saying to a fair companion —"Seek not my heart; the beasts have eaten it." Grim and wearied as he is, our poet is not above the favourite conceits of his school:—

> "Tes hanches sont amoureuses
> De ton dos et de ses seins,
> Et tu ravis les coussins
> Par tes poses langoureuses !"

And this is quite in the symbolizing style of the Italian school, of which I shall give many examples when treating of Mr. Rossetti:—

> "*La Haine est un ivrogne* au fond d'une taverne,
> Qui sent toujours la soif naître de la liqueur
> Et se multiplier comme l'hydre de Lerne.
>
> "—Mais les buveurs heureux connaissent leur vainqueur,
> Et *la Haine est vouée à ce sort lamentable
> De ne pouvoir jamais s'endormir sous la table* !"

At one time we have a poem on "her hair," in the course of which we learn (what indeed we should have guessed) that, as other persons delight in love's "music," he (Baudelaire) revels in its "perfume." He is still insatiable, and yet uncomplimentary, actually comparing his attack on her "cold beauty" to the attack of a swarm of worms on a corpse (" comme apres un cadavre un chœur de vermisseaux !") and yet crying fiercely :—

> "Je chéris, O bête implacable et cruelle !
> Jusqu'à cette froideur par où tu m'es plus belle !"

He finds delight in tracing resemblances between this marble person and his cat :—

> "Viens, mon beau chat, sur mon cœur amoureux ;
>   Retiens griffes de ta patte,
> Et laisse-moi plonger dans tes beaux yeux
>   Mêlés de métal et d'agate." (Page 135.)

But it would be tedious indeed to trace all the morbid sensations of such a lover as this ; at Paris or in the East, he is equally used up and yet insatiable; and after having tried all sorts of complexions, from the pale wax-like Jewess of the Parisian brothel to the black and lissom beauty of Malabar, he finds himself still wretched and disgusted with human nature. It is soon quite obvious that he is possessed by the demon of Hasheesh. Thoughts horrible and foul surge through his brain as the filth drives through a sewer. At least half of all the " Fleurs de Mal " read as if they had been written by a man in one of the worst stages of delirium tremens. No one certainly can accuse him of making crime look beautiful. To him, in his own words,

> "La Débauche et la Mort sont deux aimables filles!"

His crime is, that he sees *only* these two shapes on all the solid earth, and avers that there is nothing left for men but to sin and die. His dreams and thoughts are wretched. The sun rises, and immediately he pictures it shining, not into happy homes, but into dens of crime and ghastly hospitals. Night comes, but sleep comes not; and he only cries:—

> "Voici le soir charmant, ami du criminel;
> Il vient comme un complice, à pas de loup; le ciel
> Se ferme lentement comme une grande alcôve,
> Et l'homme impatient se change en bête fauve."

The gas-jets of prostitution are lit, and flare on the doomed faces of pale women and jaded men. Some few men sit at happy hearths, but the majority "have never lived." On such a night, doubtless, he composed such poems as this, which I quote entire in all its morbid pain and horror:—

"HORREUR SYMPATHIQUE.

> "'De ce ciel bizarre et livide,
> Tourmenté comme ton destin,
> Quels pensers dans ton âme vide
> Descendent?—Réponds, libertin.'

> "—Insatiablement avide
> De l'obscur et de l'incertain,
> Je ne geindrai pas comme Ovide
> Chassé du paradis latin.

> "Cieux déchirés comme des grèves
> En vous se mire mon orgueil!
> Vos vastes nuages en deuil

> Sont les corbillards de mes rêves,
> Et vos lueurs sont le reflet
> De l'Enfer où mon cœur se plaît!"

Truly enough did Edward Thierry say, in writing of this poetry, that "it is sorrow which absolves and justifies it. The poet does not delight in the spectacle of evil." Still, Baudelaire broods over evil things with a tremendous persistency, a morbid satisfaction, which shows a mind radically diseased and a nature utterly heartless. In and out of season, he invoked the spirit of Horror. Jaded with self-indulgence, he had a mad pleasure in considering the world a charnel-house, and in posing the figures of Love and Beauty in the agonies of disease and the ghastly stillness of death. As a necessary pendant to his pictures of human ugliness, he delighted to add a few glimpses of divine malignity. Looking to the section of his book called "Révolte," we find where Mr. Swinburne got his first lessons in blasphemy. In "The Denial of St. Peter" we have the following picture of the Deity, quite in the fleshly manner:—

> "Comme un tyran gorgé de viande et de vins,
> Il s'endort au doux bruit de nos affreux blasphèmes!"

And after passing in review the horrible sufferings of Christ, he concludes bitterly:—

> "Saint Pierre a renié Jésus. . . . *Il a bien fait!*"

In another poem he draws a series of contrasts between the race of Cain and the race of Abel,—in other words, between the domestic type of humanity and the outcast type, —concluding in these memorable words:—

> "Race de Caïn, au ciel monte
> Et sur la terre jette Dieu!"

—words which bear a sort of resemblance, in their foolish and reckless no-meaning, to that passage in Mr. Swinburne's writings wherein the Devil is described as "*playing dice with God*" for the soul of Faustine. Next comes a piece entitled "Les Litanies de Satan," a prayer to the evil one:—

> "Père adoptif de ceux *qu'en sa noire colère*
> Du paradis terrestre a chassés Dieu le Père!"

and in conclusion a few lines called "Prayer:"—

> "Gloire et louange à toi, Satan, dans les hauteurs
> Du Ciel, où tu régnas, et dans les profondeurs
> De l'Enfer, où, vaincu, tu rêves en silence!
> Fais que mon âme un jour, sous l'Arbre de Science,
> Près de toi se repose, à l'heure ou sur ton front
> Comme un Temple nouveau ses rameaux s'épandront."

It will hardly be contended that Mr. Swinburne has surpassed this, although his effusions are wilder and more distorted; and we may well rejoice, meanwhile, that our contemporary blasphemy, as well as so much of our contemporary bestiality, is no home-product, but an importation transplanted from the French Scrofulous School, and conveyed, with no explanation of its origin, at second hand.

Of a similar character to Baudelaire's "Fleurs de Mal" are his "Petites Poèmes en Prose," in which this cynic of the shambles touches on many themes besides lust and ennui, and touches none that he does not darken. There is here, as in the "Fleurs," an occasional delicacy of touch, a frequent delicacy of perfume, which deepens the prevalent horror and despair of the surrounding chapters. In one piece he compares the public to a dog, which flies in horror when offered some delicate scent, but greedily devours human ordure; and although he wishes us to infer that his own wares are too fine for so coarse a monster, the reader cannot help feeling that there is something in the nature of excrement in his very choice of a foul metaphor to express his meaning. Indeed, throughout all his writings there is a parade of the olfactory faculty, which awakens the suspicion that Baudelaire, like Fabullus, had one day, after smelling some choice unguent, prayed God to "make him all nose"—

> "Quod tu cum olfacies, Deos rogabis,
> Totum ut te faciant, Fabulle, nasum!
> CAT., lib. xiii.

—and that the prayer had been actually granted. There is plenty of sensitiveness to smell, to touch, even to colour; there is even a kind of perception, neither very acute nor very exquisite, of the beauties of external form; but of that higher sensibility which perceives the subtle *nuances* of spiritual life and trembles to the beating of a tender human heart, there is not one solitary sign. This poetry is like absinthe, comparatively harmless perhaps if sipped in small quantities well diluted, but fatal if taken (as by Mr. Swinburne) in all its native strength and abomination.

Here I must leave the writings of Charles Baudelaire, only observing in conclusion that, in spite of their seeming originality, they belong really to the Italian school, in so far as they are the posings of an affected person before a mirror, the self-anatomy of a morbid nature, the satiated love-sonnets of a sensualist who is out of tune with the world and out of harmony with the life of men. They are, from another point of view, the *reductio ad horribilem* of that intellectual sensualism which Goethe (in one of a giant's weak moments) founded, and which Heine repeated with a shriller and more mocking tone in his " Buch der Lieder." But Baudelaire, not content with playing with wickedness occasionally, as Goethe did, not strong enough to gibe and jeer at it, as Heine did, and too morally weak ever to soar beyond it into the clear region inhabited by both these masters in their best moments, formed the monstrous *disjecta membra* of vice into the poetic Vampire we have been examining. There are flashes of beauty in the creature's eyes at times, but they scarcely charm us, and we willingly pass away from the moral dungeon in which it lurks.

A few years ago Baudelaire died. Mr. Swinburne immediately commemorated his death in some verses quite worthy of the deceased himself. Since that period, I am happy to say, Mr. Swinburne seems to have partly shaken off the horrible influence of the " Fleurs de Mal." Although, in his political effusions, the same sterile woman of the amours is seen sitting (as Mater Dolorosa) by the wild wayside,

"In a rent stained raiment, the robe of a cast-off bride,"

and as France,

"Spat upon, trod upon, whored!"

and although the blasphemy is repeated tenfold in a series of aimless attacks on a Deity who is assumed to be a shadow, there are not wanting signs that the poet is waking up from an evil dream. The Sapphic vein of Baudelaire has been abandoned to begin with. Next, let the same writer's blasphemous vein be abandoned too. Then, let Mr. Swinburne burn all his French books, go forth into the world, look men and women in the face, try to seek some nobler inspiration than the smile of harlotry and the shriek of atheism—and there will be hope for him. Thus far, he has given us nothing but borrowed rubbish, but even in his manner of giving there has been something of genius. His own voice may be worth hearing, when he chooses, once and for ever, to abandon the falsetto.

In the discussion which follows I have scarcely included Mr. Swinburne, because he is obviously capable of rising out of the fleshly stage altogether; and I have said little of Mr. Morris, because he has done some noble work quite outside his ordinary performances as a tale-telling poet. I have chosen rather to confine my attention to the gentleman who is formally recognised as the head of the school, who avows his poems to be perfectly "mature," and who has taken many years of reflection before formally appealing to public judgment. Far too self-possessed to indulge in the riotous follies of the author of "Chastelard," and infinitely too self-conscious to busy himself with the dainty tale-telling of the author of the "Earthly Paradise," the writer whose works I am about to examine has carefully elaborated a series of lyrical and semi-dramatic poems in the mediæval manner, with certain qualities superadded which I shall have to criticize severely, and with the faults and insincerities so cunningly *disguised* that they seldom lurk on the surface in such a way as to awaken immediate suspicion.

Before turning to the writer in question, let me add a few words on the Fleshly School in general. What a great master has touched at one point of his poetic genius, has been expanded by the erotic school into a whole system of poetry in itself.

In the sweep of one single poem, the weird and doubtful "Vivien," Mr. Tennyson has concentrated all the epicene force which, wearisomely expanded, constitutes the characteristic of the writers at present under consideration; and if in "Vivien" he has indicated for them the bounds of sensualism in art, he has in "Maud," in the dramatic person of the hero, afforded distinct precedent for the hysteric tone and overloaded style which is now so familiar to readers of Mr. Swinburne. The fleshliness of "Vivien" may indeed be described as the distinct quality held in common by all the members of the last sub-Tennysonian school,* and it is a quality which becomes unwholesome when there is no moral or intellectual quality to temper and control it. Fully conscious of this themselves, the fleshly gentlemen have bound themselves by solemn league and covenant to extol fleshliness as the distinct and supreme end of poetic and pictorial art; to aver that poetic expression is greater than poetic thought, and by inference that the body is greater than the soul, and sound superior to sense; and that the poet, properly to develop his poetic faculty, must be an intellectual hermaphrodite, to whom the very facts of day and night are lost in a whirl of æsthetic terminology. After Mr. Tennyson has probed the depths of modern speculation in a series of commanding moods, all right and interesting in him as the reigning personage, the "walking gentlemen,"

* I say sub-Tennysonian because these gentlemen, with all their affinities to the Italian and French race of sonnetteers, follow Tennyson in the historical sense, and touch nothing in their poetry which he has not lightly touched in some way. The ways of a great poet lead him in all directions, into all moods, while the way of a small poet is narrow and without variety. The gain of *good* in the Pre-Raphaelite style comes from the laureate; what is *bad* in it comes from Italy and France.

knowing that something of the sort is expected from all leading performers, bare their bosoms and aver that *they* are creedless; the only possible question here being, if any disinterested person cares whether they are creedless or not—their self-revelation on that score being so perfectly uncalled for. It is time, nevertheless, to ascertain whether any of these gentlemen has actually in himself the making of a leading performer. It would be scarcely worth while to inquire into their pretensions on merely literary grounds, because sooner or later all literature finds its own level, whatever criticism may say or do in the matter; but it unfortunately happens in the present case that the Fleshly School of verse-writers are, so to speak, public offenders, because they are diligently spreading the seeds of disease broadcast wherever they are read and understood. Their complaint too is catching, and carries off many young persons. What the complaint is, and how it works, may now be seen on a very slight examination of the works of Mr. Dante Gabriel Rossetti.

IV.

Mr. Dante Gabriel Rossetti.

"Who put bayes into blind Cupid's fist,
That *he* should crown what laureates him list?"
BISHOP HALL.

Mr. Rossetti has been known for many years as a painter of exceptional powers, who, for reasons satisfactory to himself, has shrunk from publicly exhibiting his pictures, and from allowing anything like a popular estimate to be formed of their qualities. He belongs, or is said to belong, to the so-called Pre-Raphaelite school, a school which is generally considered to exhibit much genius for colour, and great indifference to perspective. It would be unfair to judge the painter by the glimpses I have had of his works, or by the photographs which are sold of the principal paintings. Judged by the photographs, he is an artist who conceives unpleasantly, and draws ill. Like Mr. Simeon Solomon, however, with whom he seems to have many points in common, he is distinctively a colourist, and of his capabilities in colour I cannot speak, though I should guess that they are good; for if there is any quality by which his poems are specially marked, it is a great sensitiveness to hues and tints as conveyed in poetic epithet. On the other hand, those qualities which impress the casual spectator of the photographs from his pictures are to be found abundantly among his verses. There is the same thinness and transparence of design, the same combination of the simple and the grotesque, the same morbid deviation from healthy forms of life, the same sense of weary, wasting, yet exquisite sensuality; nothing virile, nothing tender, nothing completely sane; a superfluity of extreme sensibility, of delight in affected forms, hues, and tints, and a deep-seated indifference to all agitating forces and agencies, all tumultuous griefs and sorrows, all the thunderous stress of life, and all the straining storm of speculation. Mr. Morris is often pure, fresh, and wholesome as his own great model; Mr. Swinburne startles us more than once by some fine flash of insight; but the mind of Mr. Rossetti is like a glassy mere, broken only by the dive of some water-bird or the motion of floating insects, and brooded over by an atmosphere of insufferable closeness, with a light blue sky above it, sultry depths mirrored within it, and a surface so thickly sown with water-lilies that it retains its glassy smoothness even in the strongest wind. Judged relatively to his poetic associates, Mr. Rossetti must be pronounced inferior to either. He cannot tell a pleasant story like Mr. Morris, nor forge alliterative thunderbolts like Mr. Swinburne. It must be conceded, nevertheless, that he is neither so glibly imitative as the one, nor so transcendently superficial as the other.

Although he has been known for many years as a poet as well as a painter—as a painter and poet idolized by his own family and personal associates—and although he has often appeared in print as a contributor to magazines, Mr. Rossetti did not formally appeal to the public until rather more than a year ago, when he published a copious volume of poems, with the announcement that the book, although it contained pieces composed at intervals during a period of many years, "included nothing which the author believed to be immature." This work was inscribed to his brother, Mr. William Rossetti, who, having written much both in poetry and criticism, will perhaps be known to bibliographers as the editor of the worst edition of Shelley which has ever seen the light. No sooner had the work appeared than the chorus of eulogy began. "The book is satisfactory from end to end," wrote Mr. Morris in the *Academy;* "I think these lyrics, with all their other merits, the most complete of their time; nor do I know what lyrics of any time are to be called *great*, if we are to deny the title to these." On the same subject Mr. Swinburne went into a hysteria of admiration : "golden affluence," "jewel-coloured words," "chastity of form," "harmonious nakedness," "consummate fleshly sculpture ;" and so on in Mr. Swinburne's well-known manner when reviewing his friends. Other critics, with a singular similarity of phrase, followed suit. Strange to say, moreover, no one accused Mr. Rossetti of naughtiness. What had been heinous in Mr. Swinburne was majestic exquisiteness in Mr. Rossetti. Yet I question if there is anything in the unfortunate " Poems and Ballads " more questionable on the score of thorough nastiness than many pieces in Mr. Rossetti's collection. Mr. Swinburne was wilder, more outrageous, more blasphemous, and his subjects were more atrocious in themselves; yet the hysterical tone slew the animalism, the furiousness of epithet lowered the sensation ; and the first feeling of disgust at such themes as " Laus Veneris " and " Anactoria " faded away into comic amazement. It was only a little mad boy letting off squibs ; not a great strong man, who might be really dangerous to society. "I *will* be naughty !" screamed the little boy ; but, after all, what did it matter? It is quite different, however, when a grown person, with the self-control and easy audacity of actual experience, comes forward to chronicle his amorous sensations, and, first proclaiming in a loud voice his literary maturity, and consequent responsibility, shamelessly prints and publishes such a piece of writing as this sonnet on " Nuptial Sleep :"—

> " *At length their long kiss severed, with sweet smart :*
> *And as the last slow sudden drops are shed*
> *From sparkling eaves when all the storm has fled,*
> *So singly flagged the pulses of each heart.*

Their bosoms sundered, with the opening start
Of married flowers to either side outspread
From the knit stem; yet still their mouths, burnt red,
Fawned on each other where they lay apart.

" Sleep sank them lower than the tide of dreams,
 And their dreams watched them sink, and slid away.
Slowly their souls swam up again, through gleams
 Of watered light and dull drowned waifs of day;
Till from some wonder of new woods and streams
 He woke, and wondered more: for there she lay."

This, then, is " the golden affluence of words, the firm outline, the justice and chastity of form." Here is a full-grown man, presumably intelligent and cultivated, putting on record, for other full-grown men to read, the most secret mysteries of sexual connection, and that with so sickening a desire to reproduce the sensual mood, so careful a choice of epithet to convey mere animal sensations, that we merely shudder at the shameless nakedness. I am no purist in such matters. I hold the sensual part of our nature to be as holy as the spiritual or intellectual part, and I believe that such things must find their equivalent in art; but it is neither poetic, nor manly, nor even human, to obtrude such things as the themes of whole poems. It is simply nasty. Nasty as it is, we are very mistaken if many readers do not think it nice. What says the author of " A Scourge for Paper Persecutors," in 1625, of similar literature?—

" Fine wit is shown therein, but finer 'twere
 If not attired in such bawdy geare;
But be it as it will, the coyest dames
 In private read it for their closet games!"

English society of one kind purchases the *Day's Doings*. English society of another kind goes into ecstasy over Mr. Solomon's pictures—pretty pieces of morality, such as "Love dying by the breath of Lust." There is not much to choose between the two objects of admiration, except that painters like Mr. Solomon lend actual genius to worthless subjects, and thereby produce veritable monsters—like the lovely devils that danced round St. Anthony. Mr. Rossetti owes his so-called success with our "aunts" and "grandmothers" to the same causes. In poems like "Nuptial Sleep," the man who is too sensitive to exhibit his pictures, and so modest that it takes him years to make up his mind to publish his poems, parades his private sensations before a coarse public, and is gratified by their idiotic applause.

It must not be supposed that all Mr. Rossetti's poems are made up of trash like this. They contain some fine pictures of nature, occasional passages of real meaning, much clever phraseology, lines of peculiar sweetness, and epithets chosen with true literary cunning. But the fleshly feeling is everywhere. Sometimes, as in "The Stream's Secret," it adds greatly to our emotion of pleasure at perusing a finely wrought poem; at other times, as in the "Last Confession," it is somewhat held in check by the exigencies of a powerful situation and the strength of a dramatic speaker; but it is generally in the foreground, flushing the whole poem with unhealthy rose-colour, stifling the senses with overpowering sickliness, as of too much civet. Mr. Rossetti is never dramatic, never impersonal—always attitudinising, posturing, and describing his own exquisite emotions. He is the "Blessed Damozel," leaning over the "gold bar of heaven," and seeing

"Time like a pulse shake fierce
Thro' all the worlds;"

he is "heaven-horn Helen, Sparta's queen," whose "each twin breast is an apple sweet;" he is Lilith, the first wife of Adam; he is the rosy Virgin of the poem called "Ave," and the Queen in the "Staff and Scrip;" he is "Sister Helen" melting her waxen man; he is all these, just as surely as he is Mr. Rossetti soliloquising over Jenny in her London lodging, or the very nuptial person writing erotic sonnets to his wife. In petticoats or pantaloons, in modern times or in the middle ages, he is just Mr. Rossetti, a fleshly person, with nothing particular to tell us or teach us, with extreme self-control, a strong sense of colour, and a most affected choice of Latin diction. Amid all his "affluence of jewel-coloured words," he has not given us one rounded and noteworthy piece of art, though his verses are all art; not one poem which is memorable for its own sake, and quite separable from the displeasing identity of the composer. The nearest approach to a perfect whole is the "Blessed Damozel," a peculiar poem, placed first in the book, perhaps by accident, perhaps because it is a key to the poems which follow. This poem appeared in a rough shape many years ago in the *Germ*, an unwholesome periodical started by the Pre-Raphaelites, and suffered, after gasping through a few feeble numbers, to die the death of all such publications. In spite of its affected title, and of numberless affectations throughout the text, the "Blessed Damozel" has merits of its own, and a few lines of real genius. I have heard it described as the record of actual grief and love, or, in simple words, the apotheosis of one actually lost by the writer; but, without having any private knowledge of the circumstance of its composition, I feel that such an account of the poem is inadmissible. It does not contain one single note of sorrow. It is a "composition," and a clever one. Read the opening stanzas:—

> "The blessed damozel leaned out
>   From the gold bar of Heaven;
> Her eyes were deeper than the depth
>   Of water stilled at even;
> She had three lilies in her hand,
>   And the stars in her hair were seven.
>
> "Her robe, ungirt from clasp to hem,
>   No wrought flowers did adorn,
> But a white rose of Mary's gift,
>   For service meetly worn;
> Her hair that lay along her back
>   Was yellow like ripe corn."

This is a careful sketch for a picture, which, worked into actual colour by a master, might have been worth seeing. The steadiness of hand lessens as the poem proceeds, and although there are several passages of considerable power, —such as that where, far down the void,

> "this earth
> Spins like a fretful midge,"

or that other, describing how

> "the curled moon
> Was like a little feather
> Fluttering far down the gulf,"—

the general effect is that of a queer old painting on a missal, very affected and very odd. What moved the British criticaster to ecstasy in this poem seems to me very sad nonsense indeed, or, if not sad nonsense, very meretricious affectation. Thus, I have seen the following verses quoted with enthusiasm, as italicised—

> "And still she bowed herself and stooped
> Out of the circling charm;
> *Until her bosom must have made*
> *The bar she leaned on warm,*
> And the lilies lay as if asleep
> Along her bended arm.
>
> "From the fixed place of Heaven she saw
> *Time like a pulse shake fierce*
> *Thro' all the worlds.* Her gaze still strove
> Within the gulf to pierce
> Its path; and now she spoke as when
> The stars sang in their spheres."

It seems to me that all these lines are very bad, with the exception of the two admirable lines ending the first verse, and that the italicised portions are quite without merit, and almost without meaning. On the whole, one feels disheartened and amazed at the poet who, in the nineteenth century, talks about "damozels," "citherns," and "citoles," and addresses the mother of Christ as the "Lady Mary,"—

> "With her five handmaidens, whose names
> Are five sweet symphonies,
> Cecily, Gertrude, Magdalen,
> Margaret, and Rosalys."

A suspicion is awakened that the writer is laughing at us. We hover uncertainly between picturesqueness and namby-pamby, and the effect, as Artemus Ward would express it, is "weakening to the intellect." The thing would have been almost too much in the shape of a picture, though the workmanship might have made amends. The truth is, that literature, and more particularly poetry, is in a very bad way when one art gets hold of another, and imposes upon it its conditions and limitations. In the first few verses of the "Damozel" we have the subject, or part of the subject, of a picture, and the inventor should either have painted it or left it alone altogether; and, had he done the latter, the world would have lost nothing. Poetry is something more than painting; and an idea will not become a poem because it is too smudgy for a picture.

In a short notice from a well-known pen, giving the best estimate we have seen of Mr. Rossetti's power as a poet, the *North American Review* offers a certain explanation for affectation such as that of Mr. Rossetti. The writer suggests that " it may probably be the expression of genuine moods of mind in natures too little comprehensive." We would rather believe that Mr. Rossetti lacks comprehension than that he is deficient in sincerity; yet really, to paraphrase the words which Johnson applied to Thomas Sheridan, Mr. Rossetti is affected, naturally affected, but it must have taken him a great deal of trouble to become what we now see him—such an excess of affectation is not in nature.* There is very little writing in the volume spontaneous in the sense that some of Swinburne's verses are spontaneous; the poems all look as if they had taken a great deal of trouble. The grotesque mediævalism of "Stratton Water" and "Sister Helen," the mediæval classicism of "Troy Town," the false and shallow mysticism of "Eden Bower," are one and all essentially imitative, and must have caused

* "Why, sir, Sherry is dull, *naturally* dull; but it must have taken him a *great deal of trouble* to become what we now see him—such an excess of stupidity is not in nature."—*Boswell's Life.*

the writer much pains. It is time, indeed, to point out that Mr. Rossetti is a poet possessing great powers of assimilation and some faculty for concealing the nutriment on which he feeds. Setting aside the "Vita Nuova" and the early Italian poems, which are familiar to many readers by his own excellent translations, Mr. Rossetti may be described as a writer who has yielded, to an unusual extent, to the complex influences of the literature surrounding him at the present moment. He has the painter's imitative power developed in proportion to his lack of the poet's conceiving imagination. He reproduces to a nicety the manner of an old ballad, a trick in which Mr. Swinburne is also an adept. Cultivated readers, moreover, will recognise in every one of these poems the tone of Mr. Tennyson broken up by the style of Mr. and Mrs. Browning, and disguised here and there by the eccentricities of the Pre-Raphaelites. The "Burden of Nineveh" is a philosophical edition of "Recollections of the Arabian Nights;" "A Last Confession" and "Dante at Verona" are, in the minutest trick and form of thought, suggestive of Mr. Browning; and that the sonnets have been largely moulded and inspired by Mrs. Browning, especially in points of phraseology, can be ascertained by any critic who will compare them with the "Sonnets from the Portuguese." Much remains, nevertheless, that is Mr. Rossetti's own. I at once recognise as his own property such passages as this:—

> "I looked up
> And saw where a brown-shouldered harlot leaned
> Half through a tavern window thick with vine.
> Some man had come behind her in the room
> And caught her by her arms, and she had turned
> With that coarse empty laugh on him, as now

> He *munched her neck with kisses, while the vine*
> *Crawled in her back.*"

Or this :—

> "As I stooped, her own lips rising there
> *Bubbled with brimming kisses* at my mouth."

Or this :—

> "Have seen your lifted silken skirt
> Advertise dainties through the dirt!"

Or this :—

> "What more prize than love to impel thee,
> *Grip* and *lip* my limbs as I tell thee!"*

Passages like these are the common stock of the walking gentlemen of the Fleshly School. I cannot forbear expressing my wonder, by the way, at the kind of women whom it seems the unhappy lot of these gentlemen to encounter. I have lived nearly as long in the world as they have, but never yet came across persons of the other sex who conduct themselves in the manner described. Females who bite, scratch, scream, bubble, munch, sweat, writhe, twist, wriggle, foam, and in a general way slaver over their lovers, must surely possess some extraordinary qualities to counteract their otherwise most offensive mode of conducting themselves. It appears, however, on examination, that their poet-lovers conduct themselves in a similar manner. They, too, bite, scratch, scream, bubble, munch, sweat,

---

* Mr. Rossetti accuses me of garbling these four extracts, and alleges that they have a totally different effect when read with their context. In reply to this, let me observe that the four poems which supply these four extracts are full of coarseness from the first line to the last, and that no extract can fitly convey their unwholesomeness and indecency. See *après*, p. 64.

writhe, twist, wriggle, foam, and slaver, in a style frightful to hear of. At times, in reading such books as this, one cannot help wishing that things had remained for ever in the asexual state described in Mr. Darwin's great chapter on Palingenesis. We get very weary of this protracted hankering after a person of the other sex; it seems meat, drink, thought, sinew, religion, for the Fleshly School. There is no limit to the fleshliness, and Mr. Rossetti finds in it its own religious justification much in the same way as Holy Willie :—

> "Maybe thou let'st this fleshly thorn
> Perplex thy servant night and morn,
>   'Cause he's so gifted.
> If so, thy hand must e'en be borne,
>   Until thou lift it."

Whether he is writing of the holy Damozel, or of the Virgin herself, or of Lilith, or of Helen, or of Dante, or of Jenny the street-walker, he is fleshly all over, from the roots of his hair to the tip of his toes; never a true lover merging his identity into that of the beloved one; never spiritual, never tender; always self-conscious and æsthetic. "Nothing in human life," says a modern writer, "is so utterly remorseless—not love, not hate, not ambition, not vanity—as the artistic or æsthetic instinct morbidly developed to the suppression of conscience and feeling;" and at no time do we feel more fully impressed with this truth than after the perusal of "Jenny," in some respects the cleverest poem in the volume, and in all respects the poem best indicative of the true quality of the writer's humanity. It is a production which bears signs of having been suggested by my own quasi-lyrical poems, which it copies in the style of title, and particularly by "Artist and Model;"* but certainly Mr. Rossetti cannot be accused, as I have been accused, of maudlin sentiment and affected tenderness. The first two lines are perfect:—

> "Lazy laughing languid Jenny,
> Fond of a kiss and fond of a guinea;"

and the poem is a soliloquy of the poet—who has been spending the evening in dancing at a casino—over his partner, whom he has accompanied home to the usual style of lodgings occupied by such ladies, and who has fallen asleep with her head upon his knee, while he wonders, in a wretched pun—

> "Whose person or whose purse may be
> The lodestar of your reverie?"

The soliloquy is long, and in some parts beautiful, despite a very constant suspicion that we are listening to an emasculated Mr. Browning, whose whole tone and gesture, so to speak, is occasionally introduced with startling fidelity; and there are here and there glimpses of actual thought and insight, over and above the picturesque touches which belong to the writer's true profession, such as that where, at daybreak—

> "lights creep in
> Past the gauze curtains half drawn-to,
> And *the lamp's doubled shade grows blue.*"

What I object to in this poem is not the subject, which

---

* Commenting on this remark, Mr. Rossetti avers that he has "never read" my poems, and that, moreover, "Jenny" was written thirteen years ago.

any writer may be fairly left to choose for himself; nor anything particularly vicious in the poetic treatment of it; nor any bad blood bursting through in special passages. But the whole tone, without being more than usually coarse, seems heartless. There is not a drop of piteousness in Mr. Rossetti. He is just to the outcast, even generous; severe to the seducer; sad even at the spectacle of lust in dimity and fine ribbons. Notwithstanding all this, and a certain delicacy and refinement of treatment unusual with this poet, the poem is repelling, and one likes Mr. Rossetti least after its perusal. The "Blessed Damozel" is puzzling, the "Song of the Bower" is amusing, the love-sonnet is depressing and sickening, but "Jenny," though distinguished by less special viciousness of thought and style than any of these, fairly makes the reader lose patience. Its fleshliness is apparent at a glance; one perceives that the scene was fascinating less through its human tenderness than because it, like all the others, possessed an *inherent* quality of Animalism. "The whole work," ("Jenny,") writes Mr. Swinburne, "is worthy to fill its place for ever as one of the most perfect poems of an age or generation. There is just the same life-blood and breadth of poetic interest in this episode of a London street and lodging as in the song of 'Troy Town' and the song of 'Eden Bower;' just as much, and no jot more,"—to which last statement I cordially assent; for there is bad blood in all, and breadth of poetic interest in none. "Vengeance of Jenny's case," indeed!—when such a poet as this comes fawning over her, with tender compassion in one eye and æsthetic enjoyment in the other!

It is time that I permitted Mr. Rossetti to speak for

himself, which I will do by quoting a fairly representative poem entire :—

" LOVE-LILY.

"Between the hands, between the brows,
　　Between the lips of Love-Lily,
A spirit is born whose birth endows
　　My blood with fire to burn through me;
Who breathes upon my gazing eyes,
　　Who laughs and murmurs in mine ear,
At whose least touch my colour flies,
　　And whom my life grows faint to hear.

" Within the voice, within the heart,
　　Within the mind of Love-Lily,
A spirit is born who lifts apart
　　His tremulous wings and looks at me;
Who on my mouth his finger lays,
　　And shows, while whispering lutes confer,
That Eden of Love's watered ways
　　Whose winds and spirits worship her.

" Brows, hands, and lips, heart, mind, and voice,
　　Kisses and words of Love-Lily,—
Oh! bid me with your joy rejoice
　　Till *riotous longing rest in me!*
Ah! let not hope be still distraught,
　　But find in her its gracious goal,
Whose speech Truth knows not from her thought,
　　Nor Love her body from her soul."

With the exception of the usual " riotous longing," which seems to make Mr. Rossetti a burden to himself, there is nothing to find fault with in the extreme fleshliness of these verses, and to many people they may even appear beautiful. Without pausing to criticize a thing so trifling—as well might we dissect a cobweb or anatomize a medusa—let me ask the reader's attention to a peculiarity to which all the students of the Fleshly School must sooner or later give their attention—I mean the habit of accenting the last syl-

lable in words which in ordinary speech are accented on
the penultimate :—

> "Between the hands, between the brows,
> Between the lips of Love-Lil*ee* !"

which may be said to give to the speaker's voice a sort of
cooing tenderness just bordering on a loving whistle. Still
better as an illustration are the lines :—

> "Saturday night is market night
> Everywhere, be it dry or wet,
> And market night in the Haymar-*ket* !"

which the reader may advantageously compare with Mr.
Morris's

> "Then said the king,
> Thanked be thou; *neither for nothing*
> Shalt thou this good deed do to me;"

or Mr. Swinburne's

> "In either of the twain
> Red roses full of rain;
> She hath for bondwo*men*
> All kinds of flowers."

It is unnecessary to multiply examples of an affectation which
disfigures all these writers; who, in the same spirit which
prompts the ambitious nobodies that rent London theatres
in the "empty" season to make up for their dulness by
fearfully original " new readings," distinguish their attempt at
leading business by affecting the construction of their grand-
fathers and great-grandfathers, and the accentuation of the
poets of the court of James I. It is in all respects a sign of
remarkable genius, from this point of view, to rhyme
"was" with "grass," "death" with "lieth," "gain" with
"fountain," "love" with "of," "once" with "suns," and
so on *ad nauseam*. I am far from disputing the value of

bad rhymes used occasionally to break up the monotony of verse, but the case is hard when such blunders become the rule and not the exception, when writers deliberately lay themselves out to be as archaic and affected as possible. Poetry is perfect human speech, and these archaisms are the mere fiddlededeeing of empty heads and hollow hearts. Bad as they are, they are the true indication of falser tricks and affectations which lie far deeper. They are trifles light as air, showing how the wind blows. The soul's speech and the heart's speech are clear, simple, natural, and beautiful, and reject the meretricious tricks to which we have drawn attention.

It is on the score that these tricks and affectations have procured the professors a number of imitators, that the small writers of the Fleshly School deliver their formula that great poets are always to be known, because their manner is immediately reproduced by small poets, and that a poet who finds few imitators is probably of inferior rank—by which they mean to infer that they themselves are very great poets indeed. It is quite true that they are imitated. On the stage, twenty provincial "stars" copy Charles Kean, while not one copies his father; there are dozens of actors who reproduce Mr. Charles Dillon, and not one who attempts to reproduce Macready.

But what is really most droll and puzzling in the matter is, that these imitators seem to have no difficulty whatever in writing nearly, if not quite, as well as their masters. It is not bad imitation they offer us, but poems which read just like the originals; the fact being that it is easy to reproduce sound when it has no strict connection with sense, and simple enough to cull phraseology not hopelessly interwoven with thought and spirit. The fact that these gentlemen are so easily imitated is the most damning proof of their inferiority. What merits they have lie with their faults on the surface, and can be caught by any young gentleman as easily as the measles, only they are rather more difficult to get rid of. All young gentlemen have animal faculties, though few have brains; and if animal faculties without brains will make poems, nothing is easier in the world. A great and good poet, however, is great and good irrespective of manner, and often in spite of manner; he is great because he brings great ideas and new light, because his thought is a revelation; and, although it is true that a great manner generally accompanies great matter, the manner of great matter is almost inimitable. The great poet is not Cowley, imitated and idolized and reproduced by every scribbler of his time; nor Pope, whose trick of style was so easily copied that to this day we cannot trace his own hand with any certainty in the *Iliad;* nor Donne, nor Sylvester, nor the Della Cruscans. Shakspere's blank verse is the most difficult and Jonson's the most easy to imitate of all the Elizabethan stock; and Shakspere's verse is the best verse, because it combines the great qualities of all contemporary verse, with no individual affectations: and so perfectly does this verse, with all its splendour, intersect with the style of contemporaries *at their best*, that we would undertake to select passage after passage which would puzzle a good judge to tell which of the Elizabethans was the author—Marlowe, Beaumont, Dekker, Marston, Webster, or Shakspere himself. The great poet is Dante, full of the thunder of a great Idea; and Milton, unapproachable in the serene white light of thought and sumptuous wealth of style; and Shakspere, all poets by turns, and all men in succession; and Goethe, always innovating, and ever indifferent to innovation for its own sake; and Wordsworth, clear as crystal and deep as the sea; and Tennyson, with his vivid range, far-piercing sight, and perfect speech; and Browning, great, not by virtue of his eccentricities, but because of his close intellectual grasp. Tell "Paradise Lost," the " Divine Comedy," in naked prose; do the same by *Hamlet*, *Macbeth*, and *Lear;* read Mr. Hayward's translation of " Faust;" take up the " Excursion," a great poem, though its speech is nearly prose already; turn the " Guinevere" into a mere story; reproduce Pompilia's last dying speech without a line of rhythm. Reduced to bald English, all these poems, and all great poems, lose much; but how much do they not retain? They are poems to the very roots and depths of being, poems born in and delivered from the soul, and treat them as cruelly as you may, poems they will remain. So it is with all good and thorough creations, however low in their rank; so it is with the " Ballad on a Wedding" and " Clever Tom Clinch," just as much as with the " Epistle of Karsheesh," or Goethe's torso of " Prometheus;" with Shelley's " Skylark," or Alfred de Musset's " A la Lune," as well as Racine's *Athalie*, Victor Hugo's " Parricide," or Hood's " Last Man." A poem is a poem, first as to the soul, next as to the form. The fleshly persons who wish to create form for its own sake are merely pronouncing their own doom. But *such* form! If the Pre-Raphaelite fervour gains ground, we shall soon have popular songs like this:—

> " When winds do roar, and rains do pour,
> Hard is the life of the sail*or;*

> He scarcely as he reels can tell
> The side-lights from the binna*cle;*
> He looketh on the wild w*ater*," &c.;

and so on, till the English speech seems the speech of raving madmen. Of a piece with other affectations is the device of a burden, of which the fleshly persons are very fond for its own sake, quite apart from its relevancy. Thus Mr. Rossetti sings:—

> "Why did you melt your waxen man,
>   Sister Helen?
> To-day is the third since you began.
> The time was long, yet the time ran,
>   Little brother.
>   (*O mother, Mary mother,*
> *Three days to-day between Heaven and Hell.*)"

This burden is repeated, with little or no alteration, through thirty-four verses. About as much to the point is a burden of Mr. Swinburne's, something to the following effect:—

> "We were three maidens in the green corn,
>   *Small red leaves in the mill-water;*
> Fairer maidens were never born,
>   *Apples of gold for the king's daughter.*"

Productions of this sort are "silly sooth" in good earnest, though they delight some newspaper critics of the day, and are copied by young gentlemen with animal faculties morbidly developed by too much tobacco and too little exercise. Such indulgence, however, would ruin the strongest poetical constitution; and it unfortunately happens that neither masters nor pupils were naturally very healthy. In such a poem as "Eden Bower" there is not one scrap of imagination, properly so called. It is a clever grotesque in the worst manner of Callot, unredeemed by a gleam of true poetry or humour. No good poet would have wrought into a poem the absurd tradition about Lilith; Goethe was content to glance at it merely, with a grim smile, in the great scene in the Brocken. I may remark here that productions of this unnatural and morbid kind are only tolerable when they embody a profound meaning, as do Coleridge's "Ancient Mariner" and "Cristabel." Not that we would insult the memory of Coleridge by comparing his exquisitely conscientious work with this affected rubbish about "Eden Bower" and "Sister Helen," although his influence in their composition is unmistakable. Still more unmistakable is the influence of that unwholesome poet, Beddoes, who, with all his great powers (unmistakably superior to those of any of the present Fleshly School), treated his subjects in a thoroughly insincere manner, and is now justly forgotten.

The great strong current of English poetry rolls on, ever mirroring in its bosom new prospects of fair and wholesome thought. Morbid deviations are endless and inevitable; there must be marsh and stagnant mere as well as mountain and wood. Glancing backward into the shady places of the obscure, we have seen the once prosperous nonsense-writers each now consigned to his own little limbo—Skelton and Gower still playing fantastic tricks with the mother-tongue; Gascoigne outlasting the applause of all, and living to see his own works buried before him;* Sylvester doomed to oblivion by his own fame as a translator; Carew the idol of courts, and Donne the beloved of schoolmen, both buried in the same oblivion; the fantastic Fletchers winning

---

* Gascoigne's verse is noticeable, like Mr. Swinburne's, for its laboured and wearisome alliteration; but the "Good Morrow" and "Good Night" are simple and graceful enough to save his fame from utter shipwreck.

the wonder of collegians, and fading out through sheer poetic impotence; Cowley shaking all England with his pindarics, and perishing with them; Waller, the famous, saved from oblivion by the natural note of one single song [*]—and so on, through league after league of a flat and desolate country which once was prosperous, till we come again to these fantastic figures of the Fleshly School, with their droll mediæval garments, their funny archaic speech, and the fatal marks of literary consumption on every pale and delicate visage. My judgment on Mr. Rossetti, to whom I in the meantime confine my judgment, is substantially that of the *North American Reviewer*, who believes that " we have in him another poetical man, and a man markedly poetical, and of a kind apparently, though not radically, different from any of our secondary writers of poetry, but that we have not in him a new poet of any weight;" and that he is " so affected, sentimental, and painfully self-conscious, that the best to be done in his case is to hope that this book of his, having unpacked his bosom of so much that is unhealthy, may have done him more good than it has given others pleasure." [†] Such, I say, is my opinion, which might very well be wrong, and have to undergo modification, if Mr. Rossetti were younger and less self-possessed. His " maturity" is fatal.

[*] " Go, lovely Rose."

[†] It is only fair to add that the Reviewer merely gives this as the judgment he was " inclined " to pronounce, only that to say so in as many words might lead to the misconception that Mr. Rossetti had no literary merit whatever.

V.

"The House of Life," &c., Re-examined.

I HAD written thus far of Mr. Rossetti's poems, just after reading them for the first time when cruising among the Western Isles of Scotland in the summer of 1871, and I had published my criticism in the *Contemporary Review* for October (under circumstances explained in my preface), when Mr. Rossetti, goaded into a sense of grievance by the ill-advised sympathy of his friend the editor of the *Athenæum*, "replied" to the audacious critic who, not being honoured by his personal acquaintance, dared to accuse him of poetic incompetence and literary immorality. Mr. Rossetti's letter, forming a whole page and a quarter of his favourite weekly print, now lies before me; and I am bound in honour to consider it in some detail.

After a preamble somewhat personal to myself,* Mr. Rossetti arrives at his first point, which amounts to this—that he is going to write a long article of self-defence to show he is indifferent. He then formally opens his case, and (that he may not hereafter accuse me of "garbling"

---

* "Here a critical organ, professedly adopting the principle of open signature, would seem, in reality, to assert (by silent practice, however, not by enunciation,) that if the anonymous in criticism was—as itself originally inculcated—but an early caterpillar stage, the nominate too is found to be no better than a homely transitional chrysalis, and that the ultimate butterfly form for a critic who likes to sport in sunlight and yet to elude the grasp, is after all the pseudonymous." Surely human ingenuity never so tortured itself to clothe a simple meaning in cumbrous and affected words! The only parallel is the author's poetry, where a simple kiss becomes a "consonant interlude," and the ink in a love-letter is called "the smooth black stream that makes thy (the letter's) whiteness fair!"

his letter) I will quote his very words, only italicising them in certain places:—

"The primary accusation, on which this writer grounds all the rest, seems to be that others and myself 'extol fleshliness as the distinct and supreme end of poetic and pictorial art; aver that poetic expression is greater than poetic thought; and, by inference, that the body is greater than the soul, and sound superior to sense.' As my own writings are alone formally dealt with in the article, I shall confine my answer to myself; and this must first take unavoidably *the form of a challenge to prove* so broad a statement. It is true, some fragmentary pretence at proof is put in here and there throughout the attack, and thus far an opportunity is given of contesting the assertion.

"A Sonnet, entitled 'Nuptial Sleep,' is quoted and abused at page 338 of the *Review*, and is there dwelt upon as a 'whole poem,' describing 'merely animal sensations.' It is no more a whole poem in reality, than is any single stanza of any poem throughout the book. The poem, written chiefly in sonnets, and of which this is one sonnet-stanza, is entitled 'The House of Life;' and even in my first published instalment of the whole work (as contained in the volume under notice) ample evidence is included that no such passing phase of description as the one headed 'Nuptial Sleep' could possibly be put forward by the author of 'The House of Life' as his own representative view of the subject of love. In proof of this, I will direct attention (among the love-sonnets of this poem) to Nos. 2, 8, 11, 17, 28, and more especially 13, which, indeed, I had better print here.

LOVE-SWEETNESS.

Sweet dimness of her loosened hair's downfall
   About thy face; her *sweet* hands round thy head
   In gracious fostering union garlanded;
Her tremulous smiles; her glances' *sweet* recall
Of love; her murmuring sighs memorial;
   Her mouth's culled sweetness by thy kisses shed
   On cheeks and neck and eyelids, and so led
Back to her mouth which answers there for all:—
What *sweeter* than these things, except the thing
   In lacking which all these would lose their *sweet:*—
   The confident heart's still fervour; the swift beat
And soft subsidence of the spirit's wing,
Then when it feels, in cloud-girt wayfaring,
   The breath of kindred plumes against its feet!

"Any reader may bring any artistic charge he pleases against the above sonnet; but one charge it would be impossible to maintain against the writer of the series in which it occurs, and that is, the wish on his part to assert that the body is greater than the soul. For here *all the passionate and just delights of the body are declared—somewhat figuratively, it is true, but unmistakably—to be as naught if not ennobled by the concurrence of the soul at all times.* (!)* Moreover, nearly one half of this series of sonnets has nothing to do with love, but treats of quite other life-influences. I would defy any one to couple with fair quotation of Sonnets 29, 30, 31, 39, 40, 41, 43, or others, the slander that their author was not impressed, like all other thinking men, with the responsibilities and higher mysteries of life; while Sonnets 35, 36, and 37, entitled 'The Choice,' sum up the general view taken in a manner only to be evaded by conscious insincerity. Thus much for 'The House of Life,' of which the Sonnet 'Nuptial Sleep' is one stanza, *embodying, for its small constituent share, a beauty of natural universal function, only to be reprobated in art if dwelt on* (*as I have shown that it is not here*) *to the exclusion of those other highest things of which it is the harmonious concomitant*."†

Thus far Mr. Rossetti; and although it is rather hard to have to refer again to poems so unsavoury, I have no option but to accept the challenge, and judge Mr. Rossetti by "The House of Life" as an uncompleted whole. A reference to this poem, so far from changing my opinion, makes me wonder at the writer's misconception of its true character. It is flooded with sensualism from the first line to the last; it is a very hotbed of nasty phrases; but its nastiness—or its unwholesomeness—goes far deeper than any phraseology. It opens with a sonnet entitled "Bridal Love," wherein we are told that "Love,"

"Born with her life, creature of poignant thirst
And exquisite hunger,"

---

* My complaint precisely is, that Mr. Rossetti's "soul" *concurs* a vast deal too easily.

† The italics are mine.—R. B.

is preparing "with his warm hands our couch;" and so intense grows the poet's enthusiasm at this information that he exclaims, wildly addressing his lady in Sonnet II.,—

> "O thou who at Love's hour ecstatically
> Unto my lips dost evermore present
> *The body and blood of Love in Sacrament!*"

—which is a pretty good beginning, quite apart from the blasphemy, for a writer in whose eyes a "beauty of natural universal function" is merely a "harmonious concomitant" of higher things. Sonnet III., entitled "Love's Light," describes harmlessly enough how,

> "—in the dark hours (we two alone)
> Close kissed and eloquent of still replies
> Thy twilight-hidden glimmering visage lies;"

but in Sonnet IV. another and higher stage is reached, for the lady gives her lover a "consonant interlude" (which is the Fleshly for "kiss"), and—"somewhat figuratively, it is true, but unmistakably"—proceeds, as a mother suckles a baby, to afford him full fruition:—

> "I was a child beneath her touch (!),—a man
> When *breast to breast we clung*, even I and she,—
> A spirit when her spirit lookt thro' me,—
> A god when *all our life-breath met to fan
> Our life-blood, till love's emulous ardours ran,
> Fire within fire, desire in deity.*"

O malignant critic, who has dared to attaint the author of these sweet lines of "fleshliness!" Let the reader examine this passage phrase by phrase and word by word, dwelling particularly on the descriptive animalism of the last three lines. Why, much the same charge might be brought against that delicious effort of Thomas Carew, entitled "The Rapture," wherein (quite after the modern fleshly style) the whole business of love is chronicled in sublime and daring metaphor:—

> "Then will I visit with a wandering kiss
> The bower of roses and the grove of bliss,
> Thence, passing o'er thy snowy Appenine,
> Retire into thy grove of eglantine." *

Sonnet V. is our favourite already quoted, "Nuptial Sleep," and Sonnet VI., or "Supreme Surrender," tells us how—

> "To all the spirits of love that wander by,
> Along *the love-sown fallow field of sleep*
> My lady lies apparent; and the deep
> Calls to the deep; *and no one sees but I.*"

There is also this dainty touch about her hand:—

> "First touched, the hand now warm around my neck
> *Taught memory long to mock desire.*"

Sonnet VII., "Love's Lovers," is meaningless, but in the best manner of Carew and Dr. Donne; and the same may be said of Sonnet VIII., "Passion and Worship." Sonnet IX., "The Portrait," is a good sonnet and good poetry, despite the epithets of "mouth's mould" and "long lithe throat." Sonnet X., the "Love Letter," is fleshly and affected, but stops short of nastiness. Sonnet XI. is also innocuous. Sonnets XII. to XX. are one profuse sweat of animalism, containing, amongst other gems, this euphuistic description of a kissing match:—

> "Her mouth's culled sweetness by thy kisses shed
> On cheeks, and neck, and eyelids, and so led
> Back to her mouth which answers there for all;"

---

* For a production quite in our modern manner, the reader had better refer to this extraordinary poem. I dare not quote another word.

and scores of the author's pet phrases, the veriest pimples on the surface of style, like "wanton flowers," "murmuring sighs memorial," "sweet confederate music favourable," "hours eventual," "Love's philtred euphrasy," "culminant changes"—all familiar enough to us from the Della Cruscans; but culminating, in Sonnet XX., with an image in which the Euphuist would have rejoiced:—

> "Her set gaze gathered, thirstier than of late, (!)
> And as she kissed, her *Mouth became her Soul!*"

In Sonnet XXI., called "Parted Love," the lady has retired to get breath and arrange her clothes, and the lover is despairingly waiting from "the stark noon-height" to the "sunset's desolate disarray." Sonnets XXII. and XXIII. are too vague for description, but Landor would have stared to see his famous sea-shell image (which he accused Wordsworth of stealing) turned by the euphuistic-fleshly person into

> "The speech-bound sea-shell's low *importunate strain.*"

The next four sonnets, called by the affected title of "Willow-wood," contain, besides the gem about "bubbling of brimming kisses," some fresh variations of a kiss:—

> "Fast together, alive from the abyss,
> Clung the *soul-wrung implacable close kiss.*"

An "implacable" kiss! Also:—

> "So when the song died *did the kiss unclose,*
> *And her face fell back drown'd.*"

The supreme silliness and worthlessness of "Willow-wood," however, could only be shown by quoting the four sonnets entire. Sonnet XXVIII., or "Still-born Love," will doubtless suggest to Mr. Rossetti's admirers other similar themes, and we shall speedily have poetry on "Love's Cross-birth" and "Love's Anæsthetics." Sonnets XXIX., XXX., and XXXI., Mr. Rossetti particularly challenges me to impeach; and I may at once admit that they are not nasty, though very, very silly. In Sonnet XXXII., however, we get back to the old imagery:—

> "Even as the thistledown from pathsides dead
> Glean'd by a girl in autumns of her youth,
> Which one new year makes soft her marriage bed."

Mr. Rossetti is never so great as on "kisses" and "beds." In spite of euphuisms without end, we get nothing very spicy till we come to Sonnet XXXIX., one of those which Mr. Rossetti calls immaculate. Here, not content with picturing "Vain Virtues" as Virgins writhing in Hell, he describes the Fire as the Bridegroom, and pursues the metaphor to the very pit of beastliness:—

> "Virgins .... whom the fiends compel
> Together now, in snake-bound shuddering sheaves
> Of anguish, while *the scorching Bridegroom leaves
> Their refuse maidenhood* (!) *abominable!*"

There are ten sonnets to come, but *must* I quote from them? Surely I have quoted already *ad nauseam*. After the sonnets comes "Love-Lily," which I have already given in full; then "First Love Remembered;" then "Plighted Promise," a lyric which I am bound to copy, as it has never been equalled since the famous

> "Fluttering fold thy feeble pinions"

of the "Rejected Addresses:"—

"PLIGHTED PROMISE.

" In *a soft-complexioned sky*
  Fleeting rose and kindling grey,
Have you seen *Aurora* fly
  At the break of day ?
So my maiden, so my plighted may
  Blushing cheek and gleaming eye
    Lifts to look my way.

" Where the inmost leaf is stirred
  With *the heart-beat of the grove*,
Have you heard a hidden bird
  Cast her note above ?
So my lady, so my lovely love
  Echoing *Cupid's* prompted word,
    Makes a tune thereof.

" Have you seen, at heaven's mid-height,
  In the moon-rack's ebb and tide,
Venus leap forth burning white
  Pearl-pale and hide ?
So *my bright breast-jewel, so my bride*
  One sweet night when fear takes flight
    Shall leap against my side."

A " soft-complexioned sky!" the " heart-beat of the grove !" "Aurora, Cupid, Dian !" I rub my eyes, wondering if this can be the nineteenth century, till the last lines, with their " bright breast-jewel," recall me to my subject. But really quotations of this sort become the merest iteration. "The House of Life" contains eight songs more. Four of them, though sensuous in the extreme, have no direct reference to nasty subjects. The other four are sickly love-poems, swarming with affectations. My extracts, however, must close with this verse from the "Song of the Bower" (Mr. Rossetti is great in " bowers ") :—

" What were my prize, could I enter thy bower,
  This day, to-morrow, at eve or at morn ?

Large lovely arms and a neck like a tower,[*]
Bosom then heaving that now lies forlorn,

Kindled with love-breath, (the sun's kiss is colder!)
Thy sweetness all near me, so distant to-day;
My hand round thy neck and thy hand on my shoulder,
My mouth to thy mouth as the world melts away."

In this and a thousand other passages one thing is apparent: either Mr. Rossetti is stealing wholesale from Mr. Swinburne, or Mr. Swinburne has been all his life robbing Mr. Rossetti.

Having so far complied with Mr. Rossetti's request, and re-examined "The House of Life," I retain unchanged my impression that the sort of house meant should be nameless, but is probably the identical one where the writer found "Jenny." Once more, I should like to quote Mr. Rossetti, in the further passages of his high argument; but he is so very abusive that I am bound to condense his statement. After vindicating "The House of Life," he proceeds to say that the four extracts given in p. 44 are grossly garbled, and printed "without reference to any precise page or poem," and that the poems themselves, if read wisely, would be found perfectly beautiful and artistic. Turn, then, to the four poems in question. The first is "A Last Confession," which describes, in Mr. Browning's favourite manner, how an Italian, maddened by jealousy, murdered his mistress. This Italian, it may be remarked, is very like our author, for, besides being disagreeably affected, he had a morbid habit of *brooding* over unclean ideas and suspicions; inso-

---

[*] Compare Greene's "Menaphon's Eclogue:"—
"Her neck like to an ivory shining tower," &c.

much that, as Mr. Rossetti truly observes, he is driven to frenzy by the real or fancied resemblance between the laugh of the harlot and that of his mistress. "Observe also," continues the bard, "that these are but seven lines in a poem of five hundred, not one other of which could be classed with them." Observe, I say in turn, that the whole poem is morbid and unwholesome, and must be drunk in as a whole to leave its full bad flavour. It positively reeks of murder, madness, and morbid lust, and whatever merit it possesses lies in the intensity of its ugly thoughts, from the first moment when the Italian began his courtship in this extraordinary fashion—

> "What I knew I told
> Of Venus and of Cupid,—strange old tales!"

—till, blinded with lustful rage, he confesses having murdered her, and tells his dreams :—

> "She wrung her hair out in my dream
> To-night, till all the darkness *reeked* of it.
> I heard the blood between her fingers *kiss!*"

In justice we should observe that a madman is speaking, but this madman has Mr. Rossetti's gift, for here is the sort of conceit with which he delights the priest :—

> "She had a mouth
> Made to bring death to life,—*the underlip
> Suck'd in, as if it strove to kiss itself.*"

With the Della Cruscan, the attempt to seem subtle and striking becomes a positive mania. What would be said of a poet who wrote thus?—

> Her nose inclined to heaven,
> *As if it tried to turn up at itself!*

Yet the one metaphor is every whit as sensible and brilliant as the other.

The second of the four poems is the "bubble" poem from "The House of Life." The third is from "Eden Bower," a production which I would gladly quote entire. "Here again," it is observed, "no reference is given, and naturally the reader would suppose that a *human* embrace is described. The embrace, on the contrary, is that of a fabled snake-woman and a snake." Exactly; but will Mr. Rossetti describe a single passage in his poems where a human embrace *is* described? The lovers of the Fleshly School are invariably snake-like in their eternal wriggling, lipping, munching, slavering, and biting; and indeed, on reflection, "Eden Bower" may be fairly considered as a complete epitome of the art of love as practised by the coterie poets. Since Mr. Rossetti is dissatisfied, let us try again. His book is a lottery-bag—we draw blindfold—but are always sure of a prize :—

> "Bring thou close thine head *till it glisten*
> *Along my breast*, and *lip me*, and listen!"

Once more,—conjugal bliss of Adam and Lilith :—

> "What great joys had Adam and Lilith!
> *Sweet close rings of the serpent's twining*,
> *As heart in heart lay sighing and pining*." *

The result (next verse) :—

> "What *bright babes* had Lilith and Adam?
> Shapes that coiled in the woods and waters," &c.

All this is savoury, and the whole poem is still more so; so

---

* Compare Carew :—
> "Now in more subtle wreaths I will entwine
> My sturdy limbs, my legs and thighs, with thine!"

that the reader feels a horrible sense of sliminess, as if he were handling a yellow serpent or a conger eel. Let me try blindfold once more for another "draw." This time my prize is from " Troy Town ;" but, before I quote, let me once more premise that the poem as a whole is fleshlier and sillier than any extract. Helen's breasts, described by herself :—

> " Each twin breast is an apple sweet !
> * * * *
> Mine are apples grown to the south
> (*O Troy Town !*)
> Grown to taste in the days of drouth,
> Taste and waste to the heart's desire;
> Mine are apples *meet for his mouth !* "

So that Paris, poor fellow, has a fair prospect of being *suckled* by Helen, and is likely, after " tasting" her " apples " or "breasts meet for his mouth," to "waste" them (whatever that means) " to his heart's desire."

But already I hear the amazed reader cry, with Macbeth, " Hold, enough !". I have thus piled example upon example, all out of one small volume of verse ; and I might readily go on quoting for pages more. I reject altogether the insinuation that my criticism was based on private grounds. I do not know Mr. Rossetti, have no grievance against him, and I can quite believe that in private life he is a most exemplary person ; but in his poetry—to go no further at present than that very small phase of a portentous phenomenon—there is a veritably stupendous preponderance of sensuality and sickly animalism. I base that belief, not merely on stray expressions such as I quoted, not merely on lines about the " lipping of limbs," bubbling of kisses, " fawning of lips " in bed, munching of mouths, and all the inordinate coarseness of the fleshly vocabulary, but on the persistent choice of subjects repulsive in themselves, and capable of fleshly treatment, such as the lyric about Jenny the street-walker, who "advertises dainties through the dirt," and is serenaded by the poet in a brothel; the poem about Lilith the Snake, and her gripping and lipping, and general arts of fornication; and the nuptial sonnet which Mr. Rossetti studiously refrains from quoting, knowing that it would condemn him fatally in all decent eyes. I said, and I say, that the very choice of these subjects is deplorable, and that their treatment is offensive; and I said, and say, that the morbid habit penetrates into the writer's treatment even when, as very seldom happens, he chooses a subject by no means morbid in itself: all this without going beyond Mr. Rossetti; but if I go a little further, and look at that phenomenon of which he is a phase, I find decency outraged, history falsified, purity sacrificed, art prostituted, language perverted, religion outraged, in one gibbering attempt to apotheosize vice and demolish art with the implements of blasphemy and passion; I find that Mary of Scotland is a biting and scratching harlot, Sappho a lustful wild beast, Christ and Christianity scandals and abortions; and pursuing further my inquiry into this phenomenon, finding religion distorted into lust, and lust raving in the very language of religion, I take occasion to say—on public grounds only, with no grudge, with no personal animosity whatever—that a number of men of real though very limited ability are, blinded by their own little knowledge, the praise of vile minds, and the applause of a heartless clique, rushing headlong to literary ruin, and dragging many of the young generation with them. What Mr. Rossetti says in explanation is only to the point in so far as it is deplorably convincing that he himself is utterly unconscious of his own offences; does not, in fact, discriminate between passion and sensuality; and endeavours, writhing under what he thinks an unmerited imputation, to save himself on the plea of personal purity and dramatic motive. No one can rejoice more than I do to hear that Mr. Rossetti attaches a certain importance to the soul as distinguished from the body, only I should like very much to know what he means by the soul; for I fear, from the sonnet he quotes, that he regards the feeling for a young woman's person, face, heart, and mind, as in itself quite a spiritual sentiment. In the poem entitled "Love-Lily" he expressly observes that Love cannot tell Lily's "body from her soul"—they are so inextricably blended. It is precisely this confusion of the two which, filling Mr. Rossetti as it eternally does with what he calls "riotous longing," becomes so intolerable to readers with a less mystic sense of animal function.

VI.

Pearls from the Amatory Poets.

> "Belial came last, than whom a spirit more lewd
> Fell not from heaven, or more gross to love
> Vice for itself." *Paradise Lost.*

I HAVE thus carefully gone through Mr. Rossetti's poetry, not because it is by any means the best or worst verse of its kind, but because, being avowedly "mature," and having had the benefit of many years' revision, it is perhaps more truly representative of its class than the grosser verse of Mr. Swinburne, or the more careless and fluent verse of Mr. Morris. The main charge I bring against poetry of this kind is its sickliness and effeminacy; but if there be any truth in my own Theory of Literary Morality, as enunciated some years ago in the *Fortnightly Review*, the charge of indecency need not be pressed at all, as it is settled by the fact of artistic and poetic incompetence. The morality of any book is determinable by its value as literature—immoral writing proceeding primarily from insincerity of vision, and therefore being betokened by all those signs which enable us to ascertain the value of art as art. In the present case the matter is ludicrously simple; for we perceive that the silliness and the insincerity come, not by nature, but at second hand; Mr. Rossetti and Mr. Swinburne being the merest echoes—strikingly original in this—that they merely echo what is vile, while other imitators reproduce what is admirable. I am loath in this connection to incriminate Mr. Morris. That gentleman is so prolific, so fertile in resources, and is generally so innocent (despite the ever-present *undertone* of fleshliness), that he may fairly be left to his laurels. He is open to the same *literary* criticism as the others, but, while often ingenuous, is never altogether unclean.

It may be interesting for the reader to compare, in a brief glance, the various poets of the Italian-English school with each other. To do so thoroughly would involve the serious task of perusing three-fourths of the forgotten English poets; for, since weeds ever grew quicker than flowers, the bulk of the poetic trash left behind by successive generations of verse-writers, from Surrey to Spratt, far outweighs the little collection of true poetry which may justly be esteemed classic and unimpeachable. But it may be observed here that all the poets of this school, though their name be legion, write very much alike. They are generally affected, and often nasty. "All that regards design, form, fable (which is the soul of poetry), all that concerns exactness or consent of parts (which is the body), will probably be wanting: only pretty conceptions, fine metaphors, glittering expressions, and something of a neat cast of verse (which are properly the dress, gems, or loose ornaments of poetry), may be found in their verses. Their colouring entertains the sight, but the lines and life are not to be inspected too narrowly." Such is Pope's criticism on Crashaw, and it will apply to any one of the school, certainly to Mr. Swinburne or Mr. Rossetti.

It need cause no wonder that verse-writers of this sort find admirers in proportion to their shallowness and affectation. This has been the case from the beginning, and it is the case now. The poems and plays of the egregious Cartwright, published in 1651, are preceded by panegyrics from all the wits of the time, no less than fifty in number, quite in the style of the Fleshly School and its Critics. Donne was the pride of collegians. Cowley was actually considered the glory and the wonder of his generation. Nowadays the anonymous press is a tremendous check on this sort of humbug, but there still linger old-fashioned journals with strings in the hands of a clique.* It is the *interest* of educated persons and schoolmen to exalt all artificial products, for they themselves can fairly hope to rival the stuff they praise and to get some sort of a position. If hothouse plants are in

* *See* Notes.

favour, any clever young fellow from a university can force them. And it thus happens that the Fleshly School, without ever reaching the general public, is in favour with the literary amateurs who yearly swarm from college, and ruin the profession of literature by writing anywhere and everywhere free of charge.

From time immemorial, poets of the Artificial School have written in the same way, and been admired for the same tricks; and indeed our modern poets can stand no comparison, even in subtle grossness, with their progenitors. Here are Cowley's lines on a paper written in juice of lemon, and read by the fire:—

> "Nothing yet in thee is seen;
> But when a genial heat warms thee within,
> A new-born wood of various lines there grows,
>   Here buds an L, and there a B,
>   Here spouts a V, and there a T,
> And all the flourishing letters stand in rows;"

which the reader may advantageously compare with Mr. Rossetti's description of a love-letter in p. 198 of his volume. The master above quoted, in his "Davideis," has the following awful passage:—

> "The sun himself started with sudden fright,
> To see his beams return so dismal light!"

This is performing a miracle certainly, but Mr. Rossetti performs a greater—he makes the "Silence" *speak*:—

> "But therewithal the tremulous Silence said:
> 'Lo, Love yet bids thy lady,'" &c. (Page 206.)

Thus sings, or screams, Mr. Swinburne:—

> "Ah, that my lips were tuneless lips, but pressed
> To the bruised blossom of thy scourged white breast!
> Ah, that my mouth, for Muses' milk, were fed
> On the sweet blood thy sweet small wounds had bled!

> That with my tongue I felt them and could taste
> The faint flakes from thy bosom to the waist!
> That I could drink thy veins as wine, and eat
> Thy breasts like honey."

Dr. Donne, however, had anticipated him in the same vein :—

> " As the sweet sweat of roses in a still,
> As that, which from chaf'd muskats' pores doth trill,
> As the almighty balm of the early east,
> Such are the sweat drops of my mistress' breast;
> And on her neck her skin such lustre sets,
> They seem no sweat drops, but pearl coronets."

These poets ever delight in the strangest and most far-fetched comparisons. Cleveland has a magnificent comparison of the sun to a *coal-pit;* but Rossetti, twenty times more cunning and subtle, sees that "vows" are the merest *bricks* :—

> "We strove
> To *build* with *fire-tried vows* the piteous home
> Which memory haunts." (Page 208.)

Cowley compares his heart to a hand-grenado; in a similar spirit, Rossetti compares the Soul to a town, and (bent to hunt the simile to death) tells us that there are by-streets there, and that Hopes go about hunting for adventures at the public-houses !—

> "So through that soul in restless brotherhood,
> They roam together now, and *wind among
> It's bye-streets, knocking at the dusty inns!*" (Page 231.)

Dr. John Donne is great on Tears : they are at one time "globes, nay worlds," containing their "Europe, Asia, and Africa;" and at another they are "wine," bottled "in crystal vials" for the tipple of lovers. Mr. Rossetti, in a semi-military spirit, thus describes a Moan :—

> "A moan, the sighing wind's *auxiliary!*"

Quite in the spirit of Mr. Rossetti's fleshlier and commoner manner, in which he talks about his lady's hand teaching "memory to mock desire," is Cowley's exquisite meditation, addressed to his mistress:—

> "Though in thy thoughts scarce any tracts have been
> So much as of original sin,
> Such charms thy beauty wears, as might
> Desires in dying saints excite!"

This is the way Dr. John Donne writes in the beginning of the seventeenth century:—

> "Are not thy kisses, then, as filthy, and more,
> As a worm sucking an envenom'd sore?
> Doth not thy fearful hand in feeling quake,
> As one which gathering flowers still fears a snake?"

Could anything more closely resemble the horrible manner of Mr. Swinburne's "Anactoria?"

It is difficult to believe that our present school of poets have not drunk deep at the muddy Aganippe of their predecessors here in England, as well as at the poetic fountain polluted by the influx of the Parisian sewers. There is a coincidence of affectation in the following parallel passages:—

THE TROJAN HORSE.

> "A *mother*, I was without *mother* born,
> In end, all arm'd, my *father* I brought forth!"—DRUMMOND.

> "That horse, within whose populous womb
> The *birth* was *death*."—ROSSETTI (p. 229).

Again, Mr. Rossetti, in Sonnet XXIX., compares LIFE to "a LADY" with whom he wandered from the "haunts of men," finding "all bowers amiss" (!) till he came to a place

" where only woods and waves could hear our kiss," and who, as an awful result, bare him three children, Love, Song—

> " Whose hair
> Blew like a flame and blossomed like a wreath,
> And Art, *whose eyes were worlds by God found fair.*" *

Nearly as absurd, but less subtle and harassing, is the passage in Drummond's " Hymn to the Fairest Fair," wherein we have the following incarnate metaphor of no less shadowy a shape than " Providence !"—

> " With faces two, like sisters, sweetly fair,
> Whose blossoms no rough autumn can impair,
> Stands Providence, and doth her looks disperse
> Thro' every corner of the universe."

Nor must it be hastily concluded that Mr. Rossetti's " apples meet for the mouth" simile is quite original.   Drummond in one passage calls his mistresses' hearts

> " Fruits of Paradise,
> Celestial cherries that so sweetly smell ; "

and in another— the following sonnet—comes tremendously close upon the *best* modern manner, minus the " lipping" and the " munching : "—

> " Who hath not seen into her saffron bed
> The morning's goddess mildly her repose,
> Or her of whose pure blood first sprang the rose
> Lull'd in a slumber by a myrtle shade ?
> Who hath not seen that sleeping white and red
> Makes Phœbe look so pale, which she did close
> In that Ionian hall to ease her woes,
> Which only lives by her dear kisses fed ?
> Come but and see my lady sweetly sleep,

---

* It is perhaps needless to remark the utter confusion of metaphor which makes a *love-act* with Life as Lady precede the *birth* of Love, &c. The language of this school will not bear a moment's serious investigation.

> The sighing rubies of those heavenly lips,
> *The Cupids which breasts' golden apples keep,*
> Those eyes which shine in midst of their eclipse;
> And he them all shall see, perhaps and prove
> She waking but persuadeth, now forceth love."

I have quoted this poem entire, because it is quite in the modern spirit, and would certainly, if printed in either Mr. Swinburne's or Mr. Rossetti's poems, have been considered beautiful; and partly because I should like the reader to compare it with the Swinburnian conception of "Love and Sleep, as known to the moderns:"—

> " Lying asleep between the strokes of night
> I saw my love lean over my sad bed,
> Pale as the duskiest lily's leaf or head,
> Smooth-skinned and dark with bare *throat made to bite !*
> Too wan for blushing and too warm for white,
> But perfect coloured without white or red;
> And her lips opened amorously, and said—
> I wist not what, saving one word—Delight!
> And all her face was honey to my mouth,
> And all her body pasture to mine eyes;
> The long lithe arms and hotter hands than fire,
> The *quivering flanks*, hair smelling of the south,
> The bright light feet, the *splendid supple thighs,*
> *And glittering eyelids of my soul's desire."*
>   SWINBURNE'S *Poems and Ballads*, p. 316.

The reader whom this fascinates had better turn to Dr. Donne's eighteenth elegy, every line of which might have been written in our generation, wherein the nude female is compared to a Globe for the lover's exploration, and the whole Voyage is described with a terrific realism of detail and daring strength of metaphor which would fill even Mr. Rossetti with envy and despair. It is, unfortunately, rather too strong to quote, though not a grain more filthy than the above sonnet. Let me turn, by way of disinfectant, to a conceit in the true Della Cruscan style, from Mr. Rossetti's works. A very shadowy Entity is speaking, in a poem affectedly called " A Superscription :"—

> " Look in my face : my name is *Might-have-been* ;
> I am also called *No-more, Too-late, Farewell* ;
> Unto thine ear I hold the dead sea-shell," &c. (Page 234.)

This passage, although quite in the ancient manner, was perhaps composed on one of those days when Mr. Rossetti goes poaching in Mr. Swinburne's French " Slough of Uncleanness," for we find Baudelaire making use of very similar language :—

> " Trois mille six cents fois par heure, la Seconde
> Chuchote : *Souviens-toi !* Rapide avec sa voix
> D'insecte, *Maintenant* dit : Je suis *Autrefois !* "
> *Fleurs de Mal*, p. 245.

Truly, this sort of reading is wearing to the brain !

I have already alluded more than once to the foolish fleshliness which permeates the contemporary treatment of even avowedly *religious* themes. For example, when Mr. Rossetti writes about the Virgin Mary, he begins in the true fantastic spirit of those older writers who spiritualised sensualism in their addresses to the Bridegroom and the Magdalen.

> " Mother of the Fair Delight ! "

he exclaims; and then proceeds with the following jargon :—

> " Handmaid perfect in God's sight,
> Now sitting fourth beside the Three,
> Thyself a woman-Trinity,—
> Being a daughter born to God,
> Mother of Christ from stall to rood,
> *And Wife unto the Holy Ghost ! !* "

The poem improves as it proceeds, but it is fleshly to the

last fibre,—quite, in fact, in the spirit of Richard Crashaw's poem on "The Weeper:"—

> "What bright soft thing is this?
>   Sweet Mary, thy fair eyes' expence?
>   A moist spark it is,
>   A watery diamond; from whence
> The very term, I think, was found,
> The water of a diamond.
>
> "O 'tis not a tear,
>   'Tis a star about to drop
>   From thine eye its sphere;
>   The sun will stoop and take it up,
> Proud will his sister be to wear
> This thine eye's jewel in her ear.
>
> "O 'tis a tear,
>   Too true a tear! for no sad eyne,
>   How sad so e'er,
>   Rain so true a tear as thine;
> Each drop leaving a place so dear
> Weeps for itself, is its own tear.
>
> "Such a pearl as this is
>   (Slipt from Aurora's dewy breast)
>   The rose-bud's sweet lip kisses,
>   And such the rose itself when vext
> With ungentle flames, does shed,
> Sweating in too warm a bed."

This is *meant* reverently, but what shall we say of Mr. Rossetti's "Love's *Redemption*," in which the act of sexual connection is outrageously and vilely compared to the administering of the sacramental bread and wine?—

> "O thou, who at Love's hour ecstatically," &c.*

Compare, also, with Mr. Rossetti's pseudo-religious poems generally, those passages of Crashaw in which all the language of passion and lust is used to describe purely spiritual and religious sensations:—

* See *ante*, p. 59.

> "Amorous languishments, luminous trances,
>   Sights which are not seen with eyes,
> Spiritual and soul-piercing glances;
>   Whose pure and subtle lightning flies
> Home to the heart, and sets the house on fire;
> And melts it down in sweet desire:
>   Yet doth not stay
> To ask the windows leave to pass that way.
>
> " Delicious deaths, soft exhalations
>   Of soul! dear and divine annihilations!
>   A thousand unknown rites
>   Of joys and rarified delights!"
>   *On a Prayer Book sent to Mrs. M. R.*

This might have been pardonable in a Roman Catholic of Selden's time, but the echo of it in a "mature" person of the nineteenth century is positively dreadful.*

I close this book of the "mature" person. I close Mr. Swinburne's volumes. I try to gather some definite impression, some thought, some light, from what I have been reading. I find my mind jaded, my whole body sick and distressed, a dull pain lurking in the region of the *medulla oblongata*. I try to picture up Mr. Rossetti's poetry, and I am dazzled by conceits in sixteenth-century costume,—" rosy

---

* Hall, in the ninth satire of Book I., took occasion to attack this blending of incongruous ideas and symbols into affected religious verse. " Hence, ye profane!" he cried,

> " —mell not with holy things,
> That Sion's Muse from Palestina brings.
> Parnassus is transformed to Sion Hill,
> And iv'ry-palms her steep ascents done fill,
> Now good St. Peter weeps pure Helicon,
> And both the Maries make a music moan;
> Yea, even the prophet of the heav'nly lyre,
> Great Solomon, sings in the English quire,
> And is become a new-found sonnetist,
> Singing his love, the holy spouse of Christ,
> Like as she were some light-skirts of the rest," &c.

hours," " Loves " with "gonfalons," damsels with "cithems," "soft-complexioned" skies; flowers, fruits, jewels, vases, apple-blossoms, lutes: I see no gleam of nature, not a sign of humanity; I hear only the heated ravings of an affected lover, indecent for the most part, and often blasphemous. I attempt to describe Mr. Swinburne; and lo! the Bacchanal screams, the sterile Dolores sweats, serpents dance, men and women wrench, wriggle, and foam in an endless alliteration (quite in Gascoigne's manner) of heated and meaningless words, the veriest garbage of Baudelaire flowered over with the epithets of the Della Cruscans.

"One moment!" observes a candid person as I write; "the emptiness and grossness of these may be admitted; but are not these writers quite unimpeachable on the ground of poetic *form*, and is that not a certain merit?" Something on this head has been said already. Let it be further said that no unsound soul is clad in a sound form; and that what holds true of matter and thought, holds equally true of manner and style: both may seem rapid and strong, but neither will bear five minutes' criticism. Imagine an English writer pluming himself on his careful choice of diction, and publishing such a verse as the following:—

> "Nothing is better, I *well* think,
> Than love; the hidden *well*-*water*
> Is not so delicate to drink:
> This was *well* seen of me and her."
>
> SWINBURNE'S *Poems and Ballads*.

Or this other of Mr. Rossetti:—

> "In painting her I shrined her face
> 'Mid mystic trees, where light falls in
> Hardly at all; a covert place
> *Where you might think to find a din*

> *Of doubtful talk,* and a live flame
> Wandering, and many a shape *whose name
> Not itself knoweth,* and old dew,
> And your own footsteps meeting you,
> And all things going as they came." (Page 128.)

Apart altogether from the meaninglessness, was ever writing so formally slovenly and laboriously limp? I have no time to pile example on example; I leave that task to the reader, who will not have to hunt far or long for some of the worst writing in our language. Of a piece are such expressions as, "O their glance is loftiest *dole!*" "in grove the *gracile* Spring trembles;" "her soft body, dainty thin;" "handsome Jenny mine;" "smouldering senses;" "the rustling covert of my soul;" "a little *spray* of tears;" "culminant changes;" "wasteful warmth of tears;" "the sunset's desolate disarray;" "watered my heart's drouth;" "the wind's wellaway;" "a shaken shadow intolerable;" "that swallow's *soar*" (a swallow, by the way, does not soar); "my eyes, wide open, *had the run* of some ten weeds to rest upon;" and a thousand others, as bad or worse, all to be found in Mr. Rossetti's small volume; besides the thousands upon thousands to be found in the works of his more fruitful brethren.

It would be wasting time to criticize details so worthless, save for the purpose of showing that insincerity in one respect argues insincerity in all, and that where we find a man choosing worthless subjects and affecting trashy models, we may rely on finding his treatment, down to the tiniest detail, frivolous, absurd, and reckless. The affectation of carefulness in composition is in proportion to the affectation of subtlety of theme; and the result is a lamentable amount, not of valuable poetic form, but of sound and fury, signify-

VII.

> "Away with love verses, sugared in rhyme—the intrigues, amours of idlers,
> Fitted for only banquets of the night, where dancers to late music slide;
> The unhealthy pleasures, extravagant dissipations of the few."
>
> WALT WHITMAN.

Is this London? Is this the year 1872? That peep of blue up yonder resembles the sky, and these figures that pass seem men and women. What evil dream, then, what malignant influence is upon me? Weary of surveying the poetry of the past, and listening to the amatory wails of generations, I walk down the streets, and lo! again harlots stare from the shop-windows, and the great Alhambra posters cover the dead-walls. I go to the theatre which is crowded nightly, and I listen in absolute amaze to the bestialities of *Geneviève de Brabant*. I walk in the broad day, and a dozen hands offer me indecent prints. I step into a bookseller's shop, and behold! I am recommended to purchase a reprint of the plays and novels of Mrs. Aphra Behn. I buy a cheap republican newspaper, thinking that there, at least, I shall find some relief, if only in the wildest stump oratory, and I am saluted instead in these words:—

"FANNY HILL. Genuine edition, illustrated. Two volumes, 2s. 6d. each. Lovers' Festival, plates, 3s. 6d. Adventures of a Lady's Maid, 2s. 6d. Intrigues of a Ballet Girl, 2s. 6d. Aristotle, illustrated, 2s. French Transparent Cards, 1s. the set. Cartes de Visite from life, 1s. List two stamps. London: H. D——, 15, St. M—— R——d, C——ll.

"FANNY HILL, coloured plates, 2 vols. 4*s.*; Aristotle's Masterpiece, plates, 2*s.* 6*d.*; Life of the celebrated Moll Flanders, 5*s.* 6*d.*; Mysteries of a Convent, 1*s.* List sent on receipt of two stamps. E. B——, 9, R——n S——t, B—— S——, E.

"THE BACHELOR'S SCARF PIN, containing secret photos of pretty women, 24 stamps; French Cards, 1*s.* the set; Life of a Ballet Girl, 2*s.* 6*d.*; Bang-up Reciter, 2*s.*; Maria Monk, 1*s.* 6*d.*; Fanny Hill, with plates, 3*s.* 6*d.* Lists two stamps. C. N——, 4, K——'s S——. Avenue, B——."

Step where I may, the snake Sensualism spits its venom upon me. The deeper I probe the public sore, the more terrible I find its nature. I ask my physician for his experience; he only shakes his head, and dares not utter all he knows. I consult the police; they give me such details of unapproachable crime as fill my soul with horror. Returning home, I meet a friend, who tells me that the Society for the Suppression of Vice has at last stirred itself, and that the Lord Chamberlain, moreover, has interdicted the last foul importation from France.* O for a scourge to whip these money-changers of Vice for ever out of the Temple!

Now, God forbid that I should charge any living English poet with desiring to encourage debauchery and to demoralise the public. I believe that both Mr. Swinburne and Mr. Rossetti are honest men, pure according to their lights, loving what is beautiful, conscientiously following what inspiration lies within them. They do not quite realise that they are merely supplementing the literature of

---

* An interdiction which, says the *Athenæum*, "is the most wanton violation of liberty, and the most unwarrantable interference with Art, that modern times' have witnessed!" It is to be hoped, however, that the Lord Chamberlain will not be dispirited by the indignation of Sir Charles Dilke's journal, which, as the leading organ of the Fleshly School, is as peculiar in its notions of literary decency as Sir Charles himself in his notions of political propriety.

Holywell Street, and writing books well worthy of being sold under "sealed covers." Much of Mr. Swinburne's grossness has come of the mad aggressiveness of youth, fostered by reading the worst French poets. Nearly all Mr. Rossetti's effeminacy comes of eternal self-contemplation, of trashy models, of want of response to the needs and the duties of his time. What stuff is this they are putting forward, or suffering their coterie to put forward for them? It is time, they say, that the simple and natural delights of the Body should be sung as holy; it is unbearable, they echo, that purists should object to the record of sane pleasures of sense; it is just, they reiterate, that Passion should have its poetry and the Flesh its vindication.* As if the "simple and natural delights of the body" had not been occupying our poetry ever since the days of the "Confessio Amantis!" As if sane (and for that matter, insane) pleasures of sense had not been the stock-in-trade of nine-tenths of all our poets and poetasters, from Wyatt to Swinburne! As if Passion had been silent until this year of the Lord 1872, and as if, till the advent of a Rossetti, the world had entirely lost sight of the Flesh! The Flesh and the Body have been sung till the Muses are hoarse again. Two-thirds of our poetry is all Body; nine-tenths of our poets are all Flesh. One would think, from this outcry, that the amative faculty was a new organ discovered by some phrenological bard of the period, and never before traced as having any influence on the human race. One would fancy, from some of our modern criticisms, that the only English poets up to this period had been Milton, holy Mr. Herbert, and the author

* See, for example, "A Woman's Estimate of Walt Whitman," addressed by an English Lady to W. M. Rossetti (1870).

of the "Christian Year!" One would swear, to hear these Cupids of the new Fleshly Epoch, that English literature had been veritably getting blue-mouldy with too much virtue, and that the Spirit of Imagination had lived in a nunnery, fed on pulse and cold water, since Chaucer's time, instead of rioting in a lupanar, fed on hot meat and spiced wine, for hundreds upon hundreds of years!

Perhaps, if the truth were told, we have had a little too much of the Body. Perhaps, if we push the matter home, it is no more rational to rave of the "just delights of the flesh" than it would be to talk of the "glorious liberty" of "sweating" and the "sane celebration" of the right to "spit." Perhaps, after all, since so many centuries of Sexuality have done so little for poetry, it might be advantageous to give Spirituality a trial, and to see if *her* efforts to create a literature are equally unsuccessful.

In answer to all this, it may be retorted—in the easiest form of retort known to mankind—that *I* am a Philistine, that I would emasculate our poets altogether, and that I would substitute for passion the merest humanitarian and other "sentiment." Well, although I fear that I am a Puritan in a certain sense, I trust I am not a purist in the worst sense. My favourite ancient poet is the author of "Atys." I prefer Shakspere to Milton, and I would not obliterate a line, however coarse, of Chaucer. I love Rabelais, and hold (with Coleridge) that he is deep and pure as the sea. I know no pleasanter reading for an idle hour than La Fontaine, no richer reading for a thoughtful hour than certain (by no means unimpeachable) novels of Balzac. I see the strangest erotic forces in the loves of Wilhelm Meister, but I admit their beauty and their worth.

I welcome Heine, and could listen to his mad laughter for a summer day. I love Byron better than Tupper, and of all Byron's books I best love " Don Juan." I reverence Hugo, and I see nothing in him that is shocking, save, perhaps, certain abominable eccentricities in " L'Homme qui Rit." I still beguile many an hour, when snug at anchor in some lovely Highland loch, with the inimitable, yet questionable, pictures of Parisian life left by Paul de Kock; and I know no sweeter poet in some respects than the egregious Alfred de Musset. To my thinking, there is no grander passage in literature than that tremendous scene between Ottilia and her paramour, in " Pippa Passes:" no one accuses the author of that, and of the " Ring and the Book," of neglecting love or overlooking the body; and yet I do daily homage to the genius of Robert Browning. I deem "Vivien" an essential pendant to that wonderful apotheosis of Masculine Chastity, which is the heart of that Arthurian epic on which the laureate has poured all his orient poetic wealth. I have praised Whitman, and hope to praise him over and over again. I know no fresher, finer work of this generation than certain novels by Mr. Charles Reade, who is not generally considered an ascetic author. In one word, I have no earthly objection to the Body and the Flesh in their rightful time and place, as part of great work and noble art; I do not see any great wickedness in the old-fashioned use of the gaudriole; and I am ready (as any sane man must be ready) to regard with kindness, and even sympathy, all work of a really good and honest author, even if it here and there, as I may think, exceeds the just limits of reserve, and becomes indecent, as sometimes happens, by sheer force of power. But Flesh, merely as the Flesh, is too much for me. I find it foolish, querulous, affected, uninteresting. I do not admire its absurd manner of considering itself the Soul. I grudge it none of its just delights, even in the way of "lipping" and "munching;" only, let it enjoy them without making such a coil about them. The world never tires of *real* passion; it will listen to Burns's love-songs for ever; but fleshliness is not necessarily passion, and may abound in natures utterly passionless. There are many other functions of the flesh which it is not the custom to perform in public, but which are quite as interesting to third parties as what Shakspere calls "the deed." Really, if we set no limit to the flesh, it is certain to disgrace us in the long-run. It has already created a literature in Holywell Street. Shall we suffer it to found a poetry in St. John's Wood?

English Verse-poetry has been, up to the present moment, almost exclusively the property of querulous persons, engaged in contemplating their own images—either in an ordinary looking-glass or in the eyes of a fantastic female. We have had a certain number of great poets who have chosen to use rhymed and metrical speech—our very greatest, indeed, have spoken in this way; but many of our noblest —such as Bacon, Bunyan, and Thomas Carlyle—have chosen to use simple prose as their means of expression; and the last of these prose-poets has very recently, in a remarkable letter to a gentleman who had sent him some verses, protested energetically that he would infinitely have preferred a good bit of solid simple prose—that, in fact, Verse is an artificial sort of thing, by no means to be encouraged at this time of day. Rough and sweeping as this condemnation of Verse appears to be, there is a certain homely truth about it. It has been the unfortunate habit of most of our poets, and especially of those we have been specially criticizing in this article, to use Verse as the vehicle of whatever thoughts are too thin or too fantastic, too much of the sweet-pea order of products, to stand without the aid of rhythmical props. Ideas too bald for prose, too trivial to stand unadorned, appear unique enough when subjected to the euphuistic process, and robed in all the wordy glitter of rhyme. If any English author, in good round prose, were to call Death "a seizure of malign vicissitude," and compare Life to a Lady with whom he ranged the world till he found a fit "bower" for nuptial performances; or if any author were to narrate for us, still in good round prose, such a savoury narrative as that of "The Leper" in Mr. Swinburne's poems, surely he would very soon receive his just deserts. Yet simply because such ideas and such stories are told in lines cut into certain lengths and jingling at the ends; solely because, by one-half the public, verse is *recognised* as an unnatural and altogether artificial form of speech, the trash of windy men is christened Art, and writers without one ray of imagination are accredited with the genius of song. It thus happens that, in the opinion of many people, the word "poet" is synonymous with "madman;" and we are told again and again not to judge such and such compositions too severely, as "they are *only* poetry." It thus happens that we every day behold the melancholy spectacle of inferior men giving themselves the airs of great men merely because they can write meretricious verses. Why, I will venture to say that there is more real genius and more true literary brilliance in any one of Mr. G. A. Sala's "Dutch Pictures" than in all the fleshly products heaped together, and yet Mr. Sala only calls himself a "special correspondent," and is far, very far, from being a "poetical" person.

If poetry—Verse-poetry—is to be anything else than an impediment to progress, if it is to become something better than the resource of feeble talents unable to stand without artificial aid, it must be more and more approximated to the natural language of men; it must be weeded of the hideous phraseology of the schools, and sown with the fresh and beautiful idioms of daily speech; and it must deal with great issues in which all men are interested, not with the "damnable face-making" of Narcissus in a mirror. Elsewhere, notably in Germany, such experiments are encouraged as tend to broaden and strengthen the resources of poetry, and to multiply its facilities; but here in England every fresh experiment in language is ridiculed and disliked, unless it be a retrograde experiment, trebling the limitations and quadrupling the affectations of ancient rhyme. Mr. Swinburne's eternal jingle, and Mr. Rosseti's affected harpsichord-melody, are admired, though they throw us back hundreds of years; but not one grain of sympathy has been shown for the metrical importations, often exquisite, of Mr. Matthew Arnold, the never-ending experiments of the late Arthur Hugh Clough (a giant who died young, and alas! has left no one who fills his place in the van of thought), and the wonderful poetic prose, or prose-poetry, of Walt Whitman. The public appears to be willing that verse-poetry should remain the property of men of talent, anxious to increase its already almost insuperable limitations; and it thus happens that our men and women of genius—such as Carlyle, Hugo, Reade, Emerson, Hawthorne—have written some of the best poetry of this generation in simple prose.*

The name of Poet was once a title of honour; it bids fair soon to be a title of ridicule. The form of Verse was at one period held to be the noblest possible kind of human utterance; but that form, remaining as it does in the swaddling-clothes of infant speech, will possibly be more or less abandoned as time rolls on by the thinkers and dreamers of the world. The word poetry may one day be identical with absurdity; and no one will jingle the cap and bells of rhyme but a fool. Is there no hope? Yes, a gleam. All the blundering and all the time-wasting in our literature have been caused by eternal posturing before the mirror. Each feeble talent has been so fascinated by his own image as to dwindle into an intellectual daisy or pine into a poetical primrose. Our literary shame has sprung from want of knowledge of how the world wags, of how men and women live and love, of what mighty forces are sweeping across the earth their angels' wings. Let the Sultan of Literature, if there be such a person (and if not, we might do worse than elect the functionary), issue forth an edict ordering the destruction of all *looking-glasses*, and the immediate silencing of all persons who introduce the subject of *their own emotions*. This would at least have the effect of driving our poets, if they *must* see themselves, to see themselves in flowing Rivers or the mighty Sea, and to wail aloud, if wail they must, to the four Winds of Heaven; and thus they might come in time to find how little account they themselves are

---

* "The French Revolution," "Les Misérables," "The Cloister and the Hearth," Emerson's first set of Essays, and "The Scarlet Letter"—all these works are "poems" in the noblest sense.

in the great scheme of nature, and how much is to be done on earth besides making night and day hideous with sensual shadows and dreams. Yet, after all, I fear there would be evasion even then; for ten to one you would find some Simple Simon of the amatory type, driven to despair by the universal destruction of looking-glasses, filling the family washing-tub with water from the pump, and pining away into a shadow for love of his own image hovering therein !

NOTES.

Page 45.—Mr. Rossetti's "Jenny."

Since the above was written, the *Quarterly Review* has spoken in very similar language to my own; and I agree with its strictures in every passage, save those which are levelled against Mr. Tennyson. The poet laureate is open to judgment, and is strong enough to bear it; but I hold it to be in all respects lamentable that he has been censured in the same breath as the men who owe to him what little in their writings is good and worthy. The *Review* speaks thus of "Jenny:"—

"We purpose to close our remarks on Mr. Rossetti's verse with some reflections on a poem which, we think, reveals characteristically the incapacity of the literary poet to deal with contemporary themes in an effective and straightforward manner. 'Jenny' is a poem on the subject of unfortunate women. A man is supposed to have followed a girl of this description to her house, where she falls asleep with her head on his knee, while he moralises on her condition. The majority of poets have, as we think wisely, avoided subjects of this sort. But assuming that success might justify its treatment, one of the first elements of success is that a piece should be brief and forcible. 'Jenny' is nearly four hundred lines long. The metre at the opening reminds us of one which Mr. Browning uses with characteristic force, but which in Mr. Rossetti's hands soon degenerates into feeble octosyllabic verse. The thought throughout is pretentious but commonplace. The moralist, beginning with something like a rhapsody on the appearance of the girl as she lies asleep, wonders what she is thinking about; he then reflects that her sleep exactly resembles the sleep of a pure woman; her face he feels might serve a painter as the model of a Madonna. We are thus imperceptibly edged on into the author's favourite regions of abstraction:—

'Yet, Jenny, looking long at you
The woman almost fades from view.

> A cipher of man's changeless sum
> Of lust past, present, and to come
> Is left. A riddle that one shrinks
> To challenge from the scornful sphinx.'

Exactly. So this profound philosopher, whose somewhat particular reflections on the charms of the sleeper have brought him at last face to face with the mystery of evil, coolly remarks:—

> 'Come, come, what good in thoughts like this?'

packs some gold in the girl's hair, and takes his leave. What good indeed? But why in that case, and if Mr. Rossetti had no power to deal otherwise with so painful a theme, could he not have spared us an useless display of affected sentiment and impotent philosophy?

"The style of the poem is as bad as the matter. Descriptions repulsively realistic are mixed up with imagery like that in Solomon's Song; the most familiar objects are described by the most unusual paraphrases; a London schoolboy, for instance, being called 'a wise unchildish elf,' while the similes are painfully far-fetched. The heart of the woman is said to be—

> 'Like a rose shut in a book
> In which pure women may not look,
> For its base pages claim control
> To crush the flower within the soul;
> Where through each dead rose-leaf that clings,
> Pale as transparent Psyche wings,
> To the vile text, are traced such things
> As might make lady's cheeks indeed
> More than a living rose to read;
> So nought save foolish foulness may
> Watch with hard eyes the sure decay;
> And so the life-blood of this rose,
> *Puddled* with shameful knowledge, flows
> Through leaves no chaste hand may unclose.'

Affectation and obscurity make the application of this difficult enough. It will not, however, escape notice that the simile is radically false, for whereas the point is that the woman's heart is alive in the midst of corruption, the rose in the book, to which the heart is compared, is dried and dead."

Page 71.—COTERIE GLORY.

That the system by which the school of verse-writers under criticism has made itself notorious is at last defeating itself, is evident from a recent article, entitled "Coterie Glory," in the *Saturday Review*—a journal which, I believe, has been more than once made use of by the friends of the gentlemen in question. The author of "Coterie Glory," in a number of decisive and perfectly well-tempered remarks, surveys the whole question, and on coming to the Fleshly School, openly admits, as if on certain knowledge, that the personal friends of the poets *write all the reviews*. This also, observes the reviewer, was the case with the once famous "Della Cruscan School," surviving now only, if it can be called survival, in Gifford's ponderous but effective satire.

"A little circle of mutual admiration contrived, by ingenious devices of criticism, to create in the outer world what for awhile looked like real fame. Afterwards we had the 'mystic' school, to which the authors of *Festus*, the *Roman*, and other kindred spirits, chronicled in full by Mr. Gilfillan, belonged."

After glancing at the kind of poetry produced by the Fleshly School, the writer continues:—

"It is clear that poetry of this order can appeal only to a limited class. It claims to be tried by a special jury of cultivated persons. This, however, is a very dangerous position for the jurors. They who have been at the pains of mastering such special qualifications, by a natural law, soon regard them as the only canons of taste; nothing which does not conform to them has the true ring. Having conquered caviare, they find all that pleases 'the general' tasteless. Philistinism itself is not more adverse to discrimination than this Pharisaic isolation. Once in this frame of mind, men rapidly unlearn judging in favour of believing; they feel that they do right to be partisans in such a cause; they taste the keen delights of initiation into a creed hidden from the vulgar; they reject all moderating or hostile criticism from the laity without, as proceeding from men not specially qualified; they tend to pass from faith into fanaticism. Hence also, the general attitude of criticism being of the tolerant or sceptical order already described, *the believers at first write all the reviews, and man every bastion of what Goethe somewhere calls the 'critical Zion.' That it has been so in the case of our later 'Pre-Raffaelites' is denied nowhere.* Crowns thus decreed may certainly and uninvidiously be described as 'Coterie Glory.'

"A curious sign, lastly, confirms the position which we have here advanced. It is the very essence of faith to be uncritical; to regard the day for criticism as passed. It seems to be simply impossible for the artist and his circle of believers to regard a criticism on his art as anything but a criticism on himself. Many of our readers who may have watched with amusement the recent squabble between Mr. Buchanan and Mr. Rossetti will recognise a proof of our statement. Into the merits of the case we decline to go; we do not ask whether Mr. Buchanan's attacks were well founded, whether he was entitled to use a pseudonym, or whether his article exhibited that good taste which is nowhere more called for than when a question of taste is the matter in discussion. Our point is, that *the 'Fleshly School of Poetry' did, in the main, attempt to try Mr. Rossetti's verses, and not Mr. Rossetti himself as distinct from Mr. Rossetti the author, by critical rules. That the poet, rudely roused from the security of fame generated by the too friendly voices of disciples, should have regarded his reviewer as actuated by base personal motives was natural. But it is characteristic that the followers should be under the same impression.* One of the latest of them has just published a further reply to Mr. Buchanan, which rivals what we had too fondly believed was the tone of discussion and the form of argument peculiar to the 'odium theologicum.' Mr. Forman, the writer, is so hurried away by zeal for his faith that, though known only as a critic, he prefixes to his paper a cruel (and in this case, we are sure, an inapplicable) motto, describing critics as the offspring of jealousy and literary failure. To re-state Mr. Buchanan's arguments in his own vocabulary appears to Mr. Forman, and we do not doubt appears in perfect good faith, equivalent to their refutation. To quote in full Mr. Rossetti's sonnet on 'Nuptial Sleep' is proof of its maiden modesty of phrase so absolute that a man must be, we cannot venture to say what, who denies it. The gist of the whole is, that every criticism made against the book is in fact levelled against the author. What reads like a remark that a rhyme is weak is really an ungentlemanly libel on the rhymester. It is obvious that this is the canon, not of criticism, but of fanatic faith; nay, that it implicitly treats criticism as sin. For what judgment is possible if critical blame is treated as personal malignity, and if to ascribe affectation to a song is the same as to insult an artist? Yet such is the impassioned spirit of coterie that this appears to be the underlying, though no doubt the wholly unconscious, postulate of the poet and his followers. We altogether disclaim such an inference; and give notice that when we say that Mr. Buchanan's attack is less damaging than Mr. Forman's defence, we do not thereby imply that Mr. Forman has a base or wilful intention to injure Mr. Rossetti. He is only what some writer calls 'that worst of enemies, your worshipper.'"—*Saturday Review*, Feb. 24th, 1872.

These remarks are worth attention, firstly, for their inherent truth; and secondly, because they come from a quarter which can certainly not be accused of friendliness to myself.

Page 87.—WALT WHITMAN.

There is at the present moment living in America a great ideal prophet, who is imagined by many men on both sides of the Atlantic to be one of the sanest and grandest figures to be found in literature, and whose books, it is believed, though now despised, may one day be esteemed as an especial glory of this generation. It is no part of my present business to eulogize Walt Whitman, or to protest against the popular misconceptions concerning him; but it just happens that I have been asked, honestly enough, how it is that I despise so much the Fleshly School of Poetry in England and admire so much the poetry which is widely considered unclean and animal in America? It is urged, moreover, that Mr. Rossetti and Mr. Swinburne merely repeat the immodesties of the author of "Leaves of Grass," and that to be quite consistent I must condemn all alike. Very true, if Whitman be a poet of *this* complexion, if his poetry be shot through and through with animalism as certain stuffs are shot through and through with silk. But it requires no great subtlety of sight to perceive the difference between these men. To begin with, there are Singers, imitative and shallow; while that other is a Bard, outrageously original and creative in the form and substance of his so-called verse. In the next place, Whitman is in the highest sense a spiritual person; every word he utters is symbolic: he is a colossal mystic; but in all his great work, the theme of which is spiritual purity and health, there are not more than fifty lines of a thoroughly indecent kind, and these fifty lines are embedded in passages in the noblest sense antagonistic to mere lust and indulgence. No one regrets the writing and printing of these fifty lines more than I do. They are totally unnecessary, and silly in the highest degree—silly as some of Shakspere's dirt is silly—silly in the way of Aristophanes, Rabelais, Victor Hugo—from sheer excess of aggressive life. Fifty lines, observe, out of a book nearly as big as the Bible; lines utterly stupid, and unpardonable in themselves; but to be forgiven, doubtless, for the sake of the spotless love and chastity surrounding them. It is Whitman's business to chronicle *all* human sensations in the person of the "Cosmical Man," or typical Ego; and when he comes to the sexual instincts, he tries to blend emotion and physiology together, to the utter destruction of all natural effect. Judging from the internal evidence of these passages, I should say that Whitman was by no means a man of strong animal passions. There is a frightful violence in his expressions, which an epicure in lust would have avoided. This part of his book, I guess, cost him a good deal of trouble; it is not written *con amore*; and, apart from its double or mystic meaning, is just what an old philosopher might write if he were trying to represent passion by the dim light of memory. At all events, here Whitman is talking nonsense, as is the way of all wise men at some unfortunate moment or other. Elsewhere, he is perhaps the most mystic and least fleshly person that ever wrote.

It is in a thousand ways unfortunate for Walt Whitman that he has been introduced to the English public by Mr. William Rossetti, and been loudly praised by Mr. Swinburne. Doubtless these gentlemen admire the American poet for all that is best in him; but the British public, having heard that Whitman is immoral, and having already a dim guess that Messrs. Swinburne and Rossetti are not over-refined, has come to the conclusion that his nastiness alone has been his recommendation. All this despite the fact that Mr. William Rossetti has expurgated the fifty lines or so in his edition.

I should like to disclaim, in this place, all sympathy with Whitman's pantheistic ideas. My admiration for this writer is based on the wealth of his knowledge, the vast roll of his conceptions (however monstrous), the nobility of his *practical* teaching, and (most of all perhaps) on his close approach to a solution of the true relationship between prose cadence and metrical verse. Whitman's style, extraordinary as it is, is his greatest contribution to knowledge. It is not impossible to foresee a day when Coleridge's feeling of the "wonderfulness of prose" may become universal, and our poetry (still swathe-bound in the form of early infant speech, or rhyme) may expand into a literature blending together all that is musical in verse, and all that is facile and powerful in ordinary language. I do not think Whitman has *solved* the difficulty, but he sometimes comes tremendously close upon the arcana of perfect speech.

UNDER THE MICROSCOPE.

UNDER

THE MICROSCOPE.

BY

ALGERNON CHARLES SWINBURNE.

LONDON:
D. WHITE, 22, COVENTRY STREET, W.
1872.

LONDON:
SAVILL, EDWARDS AND CO., PRINTERS, CHANDOS STREET,
COVENT GARDEN.

UNDER THE MICROSCOPE.

We live in an age when not to be scientific is to be nothing; the man untrained in science, though he should speak with the tongues of men and of angels, though he should know all that man may know of the history of men and their works in time past, though he should have nourished on the study of their noblest examples in art and literature whatever he may have of natural intelligence, is but a pitiable and worthless pretender in the sight of professors to whom natural science is not a mean but an end; not an instrument of priceless worth for the mental workman, but a result in itself satisfying and final, a substitute in place of an auxiliary, a sovereign in lieu of an ally, a goal instead of a chariot. It is not enough in their eyes to admit that all study of details is precious or necessary to help us to a larger and surer knowledge of the whole; that without the invaluable support and illumination of practical research and physical science, the human intellect must still as of old go limping and blinking on its way nowhither, lame of one foot at best and blind of one eye; the knowledge of bones and stones is good not merely as a part of that general knowledge of nature inward as well as outward, human as well as other, towards which the mind would fain make its way yet a little and again a little further through all obstruction of error and suffusion of mystery; it is in the bones and stones themselves, not in man at all or the works of man, that we are to find the ultimate satisfaction and the crowning interest of our studies. Not because the study of such things will rid us of traditional obstacles that lay in the way of free and fruitful thought, will clear the air of mythologic malaria, will purge the spiritual city from religious pestilence; not because each one new certitude attained must involve the overthrow of more illusions than one, and every fact we can gather brings us by so much nearer to the truth we seek, serves as it were for a single brick or beam in the great house of knowledge that all students and thinkers who have served the world or are to serve it have borne or will bear their part in helping to construct. The facts are not of value simply because they serve the truth; nor are there so many mansions as once we may have thought in this house of truth, nor so many ministers in its service. It is vain to reply, while admitting that truth cannot be reached by men who take no due account of facts, that each fact is not all the truth, each limb is not all the body, each thought is not all the mind; and that even men (if such there be) ignorant of everything but what other men have written may possibly not be ignorant of everything worth knowledge, destitute of every capacity worth exercise. One study alone, and one form of study, is worthy the time and the respect of men who would escape the contempt of their kind. Impressed by this consideration—impelled by late regret and tardy ambition to atone if possible for lost time and thought misspent—I have determined to devote at least a spare hour to the science of comparative entomology; and propose here to set down in a few loose notes the modest outcome of my morning's researches.

Every beginner must be content to start from the lowest point—to begin at the bottom if he ever hopes to reach the top, or indeed to gain any trustworthy foothold at all. Our studies should therefore in this case also be founded on a preliminary examination of things belonging to the class of the infinitely little; and of these we shall do well to take up first such samples for inspection as may happen to lie nearest at hand. As the traveller who may desire to put to profit in the interest of this science his enforced night's lodging "in the worst inn's worst room" must take for his subjects of study the special or generic properties of such parasites as may leap or creep about his place of rest or unrest; so the lodger in the house of art or literature who for once may wish in like manner to utilize his waste moments must not scorn to pay some passing attention to the varieties of the critical tribe. But if the traveller be a man of truly scientific mind, he will be careful to let no sense of irritation impair the value and accuracy of his research. Such evidence of sensitiveness or suffering would not indeed imply that he thought otherwise or more highly of these than of other parasites; it is but a nameless thing after all, unmentionable as well as anonymous, that has pierced his skin if it be really pierced, or inflamed his blood if it be indeed inflamed; but those are the best travellers whose natures are not made of such penetrable or inflammable stuff. A critic is, at worst, but what Blake once painted—the ghost of a flea; and the man must be very tough of skin or very tender of spirit who would not rather have to do with the shadow than the substance. The phantom confessed to the painter that he would destroy the world if his power were commensurate with his will; but then it was not. Exactly as much power as was given to Blake's sitter (if that term be in his case allowable) to destroy the world is given to the critic to destroy the creator; exactly so much of that enviable power has a Pontmartin (for example) on Hugo and Balzac, or an Austin (for example) on Tennyson and Browning, or a Buchanan (for example) on any living thing. Considering which fact, all men of sense and self-respect will assuredly be of one mind with the greatest Englishman left among us to represent the mighty breed of our elders since Landor went to find his equals and rejoin his kin among the Grecian shades "where Orpheus and where Homer are." It is long since Mr. Carlyle expressed his opinion that if any poet or other literary creature could really be "killed off by one critique" or many, the sooner he was so despatched the better; a sentiment in which I for one humbly but heartily concur.

There is one large and interesting class of the critical race which unfortunately has hitherto in great measure defied the researches of science. Any collector who by any fair means has secured a sample of this species may naturally be prone to exhibit it with pride among the choicer spoils of his museum; not indeed for its beauty, and certainly not for its rarity; it may be seen in every hedge and every morass, but the difficulty is to determine and distinguish any single specimen by its proper and recognizable name. This species is composed of the critics known only as anonyms. Being anonymous, how can its members be classified by any scientific system of nomenclature ? A mere dabbler in the science like myself must not expect at his first start to secure a prize of this kind; such trophies are not for the hand of a beginner. The sciolist who thinks to affix its label and assign its place to any one specimen of the tribe will be liable to grave error. In the grand pantomime of anonymous criticism the actors shift their parts and change their faces so suddenly that no one whose life has not been spent behind the scenes can hope to verify his guess at the wearer of such or such a mask. We see Harlequin Virtue make love to the goddess Grundy, and watch if we can without yawning the raddled old columbine Cant perform her usual pirouettes in the ballet of morality; we have hardly heart to sit out, though revived on so rotten a stage by express desire, the screaming farce of religion; and after all we are never sure whether it was Clown or Pantaloon whom we heard snuffling and wheezing in the side-scenes. We go for instance to the old Quarterly Theatre, confident that we shall see and hear the old actors in their old parts, or at least some worthy successor and heir to the sound stage traditions of the house; and indeed we find much the same show of decoration and much the same style of declamation as ever; but we had a tender and pardonable weakness for the old faces and the old voices; and now we cannot even tell if they are here or no;

whether the part taken in the first act by an old familiar friend is not continued in the second by a new performer of much promise and ability, remarkable for his more than apish or parrot-like dexterity in picking up and reproducing the tricks and phrases, tones and gestures, of the stage-struck veteran in whose place he stands; but not the man we came to see. We cannot hang upon the actor's lips with the same breathless attention when we know not whether it be master or pupil who speaks behind the mask. What in the elder actor was a natural gift of personation is but an empirical knack of imitation in his copyist. At least we would fain know for certain whether the moral gambols performed before us are those of the old showman or his ape. Or say that we come thither as to church or lecture: it cannot tend to edification that we should not know whom we sit under. We are distracted throughout sermon-time by doubts whether the veiled preacher be indeed as we thought a man of gravity from his youth upwards, a holy and austere minister of the altar, a Nazarite of lifelong sanctity, a venerable athlete of the Church, about whose past there can be no more question than about his right to speak as one ordained to apostolic office and succession by laying on of hands; or haply a neophyte from the outer court, a deacon but newly made reverend, an interloper even it may be or a schismatic: the doubt is nothing short of agony. I imagine, gathered about the pulpit, a little flock of penitents who come gladly to be admonished, who ask nothing better than to be convinced of sin, who listen humbly to the pastoral rebuke, accept meekly the paternal chastisement, of the preacher who summons them before him to judgment; what will be their consternation if they have cause to suspect that it is not an orthodox shepherd of souls whose voice of warning is in their ears, but a new-comer who has climbed into the sheepfold! Clown masquerading in the guise of Pantaloon; and in place of the man of God at whose admonition the sinner was wont to tremble with Felix, perhaps a comic singer, a rhymester of boyish burlesque; there is no saying who may not usurp the pulpit when once the priestly office and the priestly vesture have passed into other than consecrated hands. For instance, we hear in October, say, a discourse on Byron and Tennyson; we are struck by the fervour and unction of the preacher; we feel, like Satan, how awful goodness is, and see virtue in her shape how lovely; see, and pine our loss, if haply we too have fallen; we stand abashed at the reflection that never till this man came to show us did we perceive the impurity of a poet who can make his heroine " so familiar with male objects of desire" as to allude to such a person as an odalisque " in good society ;" we are ashamed to remember that never till now did we duly appreciate the chastity of Dudù and her comrades, as contrasted with the depravity of the Princess Ida and her colleagues; we blush, if a blush be left in us, to hear on such authority "that exception might be taken without excess of prudery to 'The Sisters,'" and to think that we should ever have got by heart, without a thought of evil to alloy the delight of admiration, a poem "in which sensual passion is coarsely blended with the sense of injured honour and revenge." We read, and regret that ever the fascination of verse should have so effectually closed our eyes and ears against all perception of these deplorable qualities in a poet whose name we have cherished from our childhood; and as we read there rises before us the august and austere vision of a man well stricken in years, but of life unspotted from the world, pure as a child in word and thought, stern as an apostle in his rebuke of youthful wantonness or maturer levity; we feel that in his presence no one would venture on a loose jest or equivocal allusion, no one dream of indulgence in foolish talking and jesting, which (as he would assuredly remind the offender), we know on the highest authority, is not convenient; and we call reverently to mind the words of a poet, in which the beauty of a virtuous old age is affectingly set forth.

> "How sweet is chastity in hoary hairs!
>   How venerable the speech of an old man
> Pure as a maiden's, and a cheek that wears
>   In age the blush it wore when youth began!
> The lip still saintly with a sense of prayers
>   Angelical, with power to bless or ban,
> Stern to rebuke tongues heedless of control,—
> A virgin elder with a vestal soul."

Or perchance there may rise to our own lips the equally impressive tribute of a French writer at the same venerable shrine.

> "Vieillard, ton âme austère est une âme d'élite :
>   Et quand la conscience humaine a fait faillite,
> Ta voix sévère est comme un rappel qu'on entend
> Sonner du fond de l'ombre où le sort nous attend.
> L'appétit nu, la chair affamée et rieuse,
> Source âpre et basse où boit la jeunesse oublieuse,
> La luxure cynique au regard fauve et vil,
> Rentre, à ton aspect, comme un chien dans son chenil.
> Jamais le rire impur ne vint souiller de fange
> Ta lèvre où luit le feu de l'apôtre et de l'ange.
> Le satyre au chant rauque a peur devant tes yeux ;
> Le vice à ton abord frémit silencieux ;
> Et la neige qui pleut sur ta tête qui penche,
> Quand on a vu ton cœur, ne semble plus si blanche."

I know not whether the rebuke of venerable virtue had power to affect the callous conscience of the "hoarse-voiced satyr" thus convicted of "the depth of ill-breeding and bad taste;" but I cannot doubt that when in January a like parable was taken up in the same quarter against certain younger offenders, the thought that the same voice with the same weight of judgment in its tones was raised to denounce them must have struck cold to their hearts while it brought the blood to their cheeks. The likeness in turn of phrase and inflexion of voice was perfect; the air of age and authority, if indeed it was but assumed, was assumed with faultless and exquisite fidelity; the choice of points for attack and words to attack with was as nearly as might be identical. "No terms of condemnation could be too strong," so rang that "terrible voice of most just judgment," "for the revolting picturesqueness of A's description of the sexual relation;" it was illustrated by sacramental symbols of "gross profanity;" it gave evidence of "emasculate obscenity,"* and a deliberate addiction to "the worship of Priapus." The virtuous journalist, I have observed, is remarkably fond of Priapus; his frequent and forcible allusions to "the honest garden-god" recur with a devout iteration to be found in no other worshipper; for one such reference in graver or lighter verse you may find a score in prose of the moral and critical sort. Long since, in that incomparable satiric essay which won for its young author the deathless

---

* "*Climène.* Il a une obscénité qui n'est pas supportable.
Elise. Comment dites-vous ce mot-là, madame?
Climène. Obscénité, madame.
Elise. Ah! mon Dieu! obscénité. Je ne sais ce que ce mot veut dire; mais je le trouve le plus joli du monde."
MOLIERE, *La Critique de l'Ecole des Femmes*, sc. 3.

applause of Balzac — "magnifique préface d'un livre magnifique"—Théophile Gautier had occasion to remark on the intimate familiarity of the virtuous journalist with all the occult obscenities of literature, the depth and width of range which his studies in that line would seem to have taken, if we might judge by his numerous and ready citations of the titles of indecent books with which he would associate the title of the book reviewed. This problematic intimacy the French poet finds no plausible way to explain; and with it we must leave the other problem on which I have touched above, in the hope that some day a more advanced stage of scientific inquiry will produce men competent to resolve it. Meantime we may remark again the very twang of the former preacher in the voice which now denounces to our ridicule B's "want of sense," while it invokes our disgust as fire from heaven on his "want of decency," in the use of a type borrowed from the Christian mythology and applied to actual doings and sufferings; and once more we surely seem to "know the sweet Roman hand" that sets down our errors in its register, when the critic remarks on the absurd inconsequence of a poet who addresses by name and denounces in person a god in whose personal existence he does not believe. In the name of all divine persons that ever did or did not exist, what on earth or in heaven would the critic in such a case expect? Is it from the believers in a particular god or gods that he would look for exposure and denunciation of their especial creed? Would it be natural and rational for a man to attack and denounce a name he believes in or a person he adores, unnatural and irrational to attack and denounce by name a godhead or a gospel he finds incredible and abominable to him? When a great poetess apostrophized the gods of Hellas as dead, was the form of apostrophe made inconsequent and absurd by the fact that she did not believe them to be alive? For a choicer specimen of preacher's logic than this we might seek long without finding it. But we must not be led away into argument or answer addressed to the subjects of our research, while as yet the work before us remains unaccomplished. The self-imposed task is simple and severe; we would merely submit to the analysis of scientific examination the examiners of other men; bring under our microscope, as it were, the telescopic apparatus which they on their side bring to investigate from below things otherwise invisible to them, as they would be imperceptible from above but for the microscopic lens which science enables us in turn to apply to themselves and their appliances. As to answer, if any workman who has done any work of his own should be asked why he does not come forward to take up any challenge flung down to him, or sweep out of his way any litter of lies and insults that may chance to encumber it for a moment, his reply for his fellows and himself to those who suggest that they should engage in such a warfare might perhaps run somewhat thus: Are we cranes or mice, that we should give battle to the frogs or the pigmies? Examine them we may at our leisure, in the pursuit of natural history, if our studies should chance to have taken that turn; but as we cannot, when they speak out of the darkness, tell frog from frog by his croak, or pigmy from pigmy by his features, and are thus liable at every moment to the most unscientific errors in definition, it seems best to seek no further for quaint or notable examples of a kind which we cannot profitably attempt to classify. Not without regret, therefore, we resign to more adventurous explorers the whole range of the anonymous wilderness, and confine our own modest researches to the limits within which we may trust ourselves to make no grave mistakes of kind. But within these limits, too, there is a race which defies even scientific handling, and for a reason yet graver and more final. Among writers who publish and sign such things as they have to say about or against their contemporaries, there is still, as of old, a class which is protected against response or remark, as (to use an apt example of Macaulay's) "the skunk is protected against the hunters. It is safe, because it is too filthy to handle, and too noisome even to approach." To this class belong the creatures known to naturalists by the generic term of coprophagi; a generation which derives its sustenance from the unclean matter which produced it, and lives on the very stuff of which it was born:

> "They are no vipers, yet they feed
> On mother-dung which did them breed:"

and under this head we find ranked, for example, the workers and dealers in false and foul ware for minor magazines and newspapers, to whom now that they know their ears to be safe from the pillory and their shoulders from the scourge there is no restraint and no reply applicable but the restraint and the reply of the law which imposes on their kind the brand of a shameful penalty; and it is not every day that an honest man will care to come forward and procure its infliction on some representative rascal of the tribe at the price of having to swear that the spittle aimed at his face came from the lips of a liar; that he has not lived on such terms of intimacy with the honest gentleman at the bar that the confidential and circumstantial report given of his life and opinions, habits and theories, person and conversation, is absolutely to be taken for gospel by the curious in such matters. The age of Pope is past, and we no longer expect a man of note to dive into the common sink of letters for the purpose of unearthing from its native place and nailing up by the throat in sight of day any chance vermin that may slink out in foul weather to assail him. The celebrity of Oldmixon and Curll is no longer attainable by dint of scurrilous persistency in provocation; in vain may the sons of the sewer look up with longing eyes after the hope of such peculiar immortality as that bestowed by Swift on the names of Whiston and Ditton: upon their upturned faces there will fall no drop or flake of such unfragrant fame. When some one told Dr. Johnson that a noted libeller had been publicly kicked in the streets of Dublin, his answer was to the effect that he was glad to hear of so clever a man rising so rapidly in the world; when he was in London, no one at whom his personalities might be launched ever thought it worth while to kick him. There are writers apparently consumed by a vain ambition to emulate the rise in life thus achieved by one of their precursors; and it takes them some time to discover, and despond as they admit, that such luck is not always to be looked for. Some, as in fond hope of such notice, assume the gay patrician in their style, while others in preference affect the honest plebeian; but in neither case do they succeed in attracting the touch which might confer celebrity; the very means they take to draw it down on themselves suffice to keep it off; at each fresh emanation or exhalation of their malodorous souls it becomes more clearly impossible for man to approach them even "with stopped nostril and glove-guarded hand." When the dirtier lackeys of literature come forward in cast clothes to revile or to represent their betters, to caricature by personation or by defamation the masters of the house, men do not now look at them and pass by; they pass without looking, and have neither eye for the pretentions nor cudgel for the backs of the Marquis de Mascarille and the Vicomte de Jodelet.

Of such creatures, then, even though they be nothing if not critical, we do not propose to treat; but only of such examples of the critical kind as may be shown in public without apology by the collector, not retained (if retained at all) for necessary purposes of science on the most private shelves of his cabinet. Among these more presentable classes there is considerable diversity of kind to be traced by the discerning eye, though many signs and symptoms be in almost all cases identical. There is the critic who believes that no good thing can come out of such a Nazarene generation as the men of his own time; and there is the critic who believes first in himself alone, and through himself in the gods or godlings of his worship and the eggs or nestlings hatched or addled under the incubation of his patronage. Between these two kinds there rages a natural warfare as worthy of a burlesque poet as any batrachomyomachy that ever was fought out. It is no bad sport to watch through a magnifying glass the reciprocal attack and defence of their little lines of battle and posts of vantage—

> " Et, dans la goutte d'eau, les guerres du volvoce
> Avec le vibrion."

In all times there have been men in plenty convinced of the decadence of their own age ; of which they have not usually been classed among the more distinguished children. We are happy in having among us a critic of some culture and of much noisy pertinacity who will serve well enough to represent the tribe. I distinguish his book on " The Poetry of the Period," supplemented as I take it to be by further essays in criticism thrown out in the same line, not for any controversial purpose, and assuredly with no view of attempting to answer or to confute the verdicts therein issued, to prove by force of reasoning or proclaim by force of rhetoric that the gulf between past and present is less deep and distinct than this author believes and alleges it to be ; that the dead were not so far above the average type of men, that the living are not so far below it, as writers of this type have always been equally prone to maintain. I have little taste for such controversy and little belief in its value ; but even if the diversion of arguing as to what sort of work should be done or is being done or has been were in my mind preferable to the business of doing as seems to me best whatever work my hand finds to do, I should not enter into a debate in which my own name was mixed up. Whether the men of this time be men of a great age or a small is not a matter to be decided by their own assertion or denial; but in any case a man of any generation can keep his hand and foot out of the perpetual wrangle and jangle of "the petty fools of rhyme who shriek and sweat in pigmy jars," which recur in every age of literature with a pitiful repetition of the same cries and catchwords. I could never understand, and certainly I could never admire, the habit of mind or the form of energy which finds work and vent in demonstration or proclamation of the incompetence for all good of other men; but much less can I admire or understand the impulse which would thrust a man forward to shriek out in reply some assertion of his own injured merit and the value of the work which he for instance has done for the world even in this much maligned generation. No man can prove or disprove his own worth except by his own work; and is it after all so grave a question to determine whether the merit of that be more or less? The world in its time will not want for great men, though he in his time be never so small; and if, small or great, he be a man of any courage or of any sense, he will find comfort and delight enough to last his time in the quite unmistakeably and indubitably great work of other men past or present, without any such irritable prurience of appetite for personal fame or hankering retrospection of regret for any foiled ambitions of his own. This temper of mind, which all men should be able to attain, must preserve him from the unprofitable and ignoble sufferings of fools and cowards; and self-contempt, the appointed scourge of all envious egotists, will have no sting for him. And once aware that his actual merit or demerit is no such mighty matter in the world's eye, and the success or failure of his own life's work in any line of thought or action is probably not of any incalculable importance to his own age or the next, the man who has learnt not to care overmuch about his real rank and relation to other workmen as greater or less than they, will hardly trouble himself overmuch about the opinions held or expressed as to that rank and relation. What is said of him must be either true or false; if false, he would simply be a fool—if true, he would also be a coward—to wish it unsaid; for a lie in the end hurts none but the liar, and a truth is at all times profitable to all. In any case then it can do him no damage; for good work and worthy to last is indestructible; and to destroy with all due speed any destructible person or book not worthy to last is no injury to any one whatever, but the greatest service that can be done

to the book and the writer themselves, not less—
nay perhaps much more—than to the rest of the
poor world which has no mind to be "pestered
with such water-flies—diminutives of nature." In
a word, whatever is fit to live is safe to live, and
whatever is not fit to live is sure to die, though all
men should swear and struggle to the contrary;
and it is hard to say which of these is the more
consoling certainty. I shall not, therefore, select
any book for refutation of its principle, but
merely for examination of its argument; my only
aim being to test by this simplest of means what
may be its purport and its weight. I find for
instance that Mr. Austin, satirist and critic by profession, writing with a plain emphatic energy and
decision which make his essays on the poetry of
the period easily and pleasantly readable by
students of the minute, maintains throughout his
book the opposition between two leading figures;
the same figures since chosen for the same purpose
by the venerable monitor at whose feet we have
already sat attentive and shrunk rebuked. In
Byron the mighty past and in Tennyson the
petty present is incarnate; other giants of less
prominence are ranked behind the former, other
pigmies of less proportion are gathered about the
latter; but throughout it is assumed that no fairer
example than either could be found of the bes
that his age had to show. We may admit for a

moment the assumption that Byron was as indisputably at the head of his own generation, as indisputably its fittest and fullest representative, as we all allow Mr. Tennyson to be of his; and this assumption we may admit, because Mr. Austin is so good and complete a type of one class of the great critical kind, that by such a concession we may enable ourselves to get a clear view and a firm grasp of some definable principles of criticism; and thus to examine as we proposed the arguments on which these are based, and which we approach with no prepense design or premeditated aim to corroborate or to confute them, but simply to investigate. With a writer less clear and less forcible in purpose and in style we might not hope to get sight or hold of any principle at all; but this one, right or wrong and wise or unwise, at least does not babble to no purpose whatever like the "blind mouths" that prattle by mere chance of impulse or of habit. First then we observe that he offers us samples of either poet's work with a great show of fairness in the choice of representative passages; he bids us, like a new Hamlet rebuking the weakness and the shame of his mother-age, look here upon this picture and on this; and a counterfeit presentment it is indeed that he shows us. Taking an instance from his final essay, the summary and result of the book, we find a few lines from a slight poem of Mr. Tennyson's extreme youth, and one which is by no means a fair example of even his earliest manner, set against the most famous and the finest passage but one in "Childe Harold"—the description of an Alpine thunderstorm. With equal justice and with equal profit we might pick out the worst refuse of dolorous doggrel from the rubbish-heaps of "Hours of Idleness" or "Hebrew Melodies"—say that version of the 137th Psalm so admirably parodied by Landor, of which the indignant shade of Hopkins might howl rejection, while the milder ghost of Brady would dissolve in air if accused of it—that or such another rag or shard of verse from the sweepings of Byron's bad work—and set it against the majestic close of the "Lotus-eaters" or some passage of most finished exaltation from "In Memoriam." But the critic has yet a better trick than this, ingenious and ingenuous as it is, to pervert the judgment of those who might chance to take his evidence on trust. He has copied accurately the short passage chosen to show the immature genius of Tennyson at its feeblest; but the longer passage chosen, and very well chosen, to show the mature genius of Byron at its mightiest, he has been careful to alter and improve by the studious and judicious excision of two whole intervening stanzas; the second good in itself, but introduced by one stolen from Coleridge and deformed almost past recognition from a thing of supreme and perfect beauty into a formless and tuneless mass of clumsy verbosity and floundering incoherence. Even thus garbled and disembowelled, the passage, noble and delightful as in the main it is, stands yet defaced by two lines which no poet of the first order could have committed; two lines showing such hideous deficiency of instinct, such helpless want of the imaginative sense which in the highest poets is as strong and as sure to preserve from error as to impel towards perfection, that any man with an inner ear for that twin-born music of coequal thought and word without which there is no high poetry possible, must feel with all regret that here is not one of the poets who can be trusted by those who would enjoy them; but one who at the highest and smoothest of his full-winged flight is liable to some horrible collapse or flap of a dislocated pinion. The first offence is that monstrous simile—monstrous at once and mean—of "the light of a dark eye in woman," which must surely have been stolen from Hayley; if even the author of the "Triumphs of Temper" can ever have thought a woman's eye an apt and noble likeness for the whole heaven of night in storm. This is the true sign of flawed or defective imagination; that a man should think, because the comparison of a woman's eye to a stormy night may be striking and ennobling, therefore the inverted comparison of a stormy night to a woman's eye must also be proper and impressive. The second offence is yet worse; it is that incomparable phrase of the mountains "rejoicing o'er a young earthquake's birth," which again I should conjecture to have been borrowed from Elkanah Settle; it is really much in the manner of some lines cited from that poet by Scott in his notes on Dryden. A young earthquake! why not a young toothache, a young spasm, or a young sneeze? We see the difference between sense and nonsense, pure imagination and mere turbid energy, when we turn to a phrase of Shelley's on the same subject.

> "Is this the scene
> Where the old earthquake-demon taught her young
> Ruin?"

There is a symbol conceivable by the mind's eye, noble and coherent. But to such critics as Mr. Austin it is all one; for them there are no such fine-drawn distinctions between words with a meaning and words without—with them, as with poor Elkanah, "if they rhyme and rattle, all is well." This selection and collocation of fragmentary passages, it will be said, is not the best way to attain a fair and serious estimate of either poet's worth or station; Byron may be or may not be as much greater than Tennyson as the critic shall please, but this is not a sufficient process of proof. Nor assuredly do I think it is; but the method chosen is none of mine; it is the method chosen by the critic whom for the moment I follow to examine his system of criticism. His choice of an instance is designedly injurious to the poet whom it shows at his weakest; but it seems to me, however undesignedly, not much less injurious to the poet whom it shows at his strongest. Such is frequently the effect of such tactics, the net result and upshot of such an advocate's good intentions. It will hardly be supposed that I have dwelt with any delight on the disparaging scrutiny of an otherwise admirable extract from a poet in whose praise I should have said enough elsewhere to stand clear of any possible charge of injustice or incompetence to enjoy his glorious and ardent genius; I have dwelt indeed with a genuine delight on a task far different from this—the task of praising with all my might, and if with superfluous yet certainly with sincere expression, his magnificent quality of communion with the great things of nature and translation of the joyous and terrible sense they give us of her living infinity, which has been given in like degree to no living poet but one greater far than Byron—the author of the *Contemplations* and the *Légende des Siècles*. This tribute, however inadequate and however unnecessary, was paid to the memory of Byron before ever his latest English panegyrist laid lance in rest against all comers in defence of his fame; using meantime that fame as a stalking-horse behind which to shoot at the fame of others. And as to his assumed office of spokesman on behalf of Byron—a very noble office it would be if there were any need or place for it—we cannot but ask who gave him his credentials as advocate or apologist for a poet whose fame was to all seeming as secure as any man's? Is the name of Byron fallen so low that such a style of advocacy and such a class of counsel must be sought out to revive its drooping credit and refresh its withered honours? *Quis vituperavit?* Has any one attacked his noble memory as a poet or a man, except here and there a journalist of the tribe of Levi or Tartuffe, or a blatant Bassarid of Boston, a rampant Mænad of Massachusetts? To wipe off the froth of falsehood from the foaming lips of inebriated virtue, when fresh from the sexless orgies of morality and reeling from the delirious riot of religion, may doubtless be a charitable office; but it is no proof of critical sense or judgment to set about the vindication of a great man as though his repute could by any chance be widely or durably affected by the confidences exchanged in the most secret place and hour of their sacred rites, far from the clamour of public halls and platforms made hoarse with holiness,

Ubi sacra sancta acutis ululatibus agitant,

between two whispering priestesses of whatever god presides over the most vicious parts of virtue, the most shameless rites of modesty, the most rancorous forms of forgiveness—the very Floralia of evangelical faith and love. That two such spirits, naked and not ashamed, should so have met and mingled in the communion of calumny, have taken each with devout avidity her part in the obscene sacrament of hate, her share in the graceless eucharist of evil-speaking, is not more wonderful or more important than that the elder devotee should have duped the younger into a belief that she alone had been admitted to partake of a fouler feast than that eaten in mockery at a witch's sabbath, a wafer more impure from a table more unspeakably polluted—the bread of slander from the altar of madness or malignity, the bitter poison of a shrine on which the cloven tongue of hell-fire might ever be expected to reappear with the return of some infernal Pentecost. All this is as natural and as insignificant as that the younger priestess on her part should since have trafficked in the unhallowed elements of their common and unclean mystery, have revealed for hire the unsacred secrets of no Eleusinian initiation. To whom can it matter that such a plume-plucked Celæno as this should come with all the filth and flutter of her kind to defile a grave which is safe and high enough above the abomination of her approach? Not, I should have thought, to those who hold most in honour all that was worthiest of men's honour in Byron. Surely he needs no defence against this posthumous conjugal effusion at second-hand of such a venomous and virulent charity as might shame the veriest Christian to have shown. And who else speaks evil of him but now and then some priest or pedagogue, frocked or unfrocked, in lecture or review? It should be remembered that a warfare carried into such quarters can bring honour or profit to no man. We are not accustomed to give back railing for railing that is flung at us from the pulpit or the street-corner. In the church as in the highway, the skirt significant of sex, be it surpliced or draggle-tailed, should suffice to protect the wearer from any reciprocity of vituperation. If it should ever be a clerical writer, whether of the regular or the secular order—an amateur who officiates by choice or by chance, or a registered official whose services are duly salaried—that may happen to review a book in which you may happen to have touched unawares on some naked nerve of his religious feeling or professional faith, you are not moved to any surprise or anger that he should liken you to a boy rolling in a puddle, or laugh at you in pity as he throws aside in disgust the proof of your fatuous ignorance; you know that this is the rhetoric or the reasoning of his kind, and that he means by it no more than a street-walker means by her curse as you pass by without response to her addresses;

you remember that both alike may claim the freedom of the trade, and would as soon turn back to notice the one salutation as the other. Priests and prostitutes are a privileged class. Half of that axiom was long since laid down by Shelley; and it is not from any such quarter that he probably would have thought the fame of his friend in any such danger as to require much demonstration of championship. The worst enemies of Byron, as of all his kind, are not to be sought among such as these. They are his enemies who extol him for gifts which he had not and work which he could not do; who by dint of praising him for such qualities as were wanting to his genius call the attention of all men to his want of them; who are not content to pay all homage to his unsurpassed energy, his fiery eloquence, his fitful but gigantic force of spirit, his troubled but triumphant strength of soul; to his passionate courage, his noble wrath and pity and scorn, his bright and burning wit, the invincible vitality and sleepless vigour of action and motion which informs and imbues for us all his better part of work as with a sense of living and personal power; who are dissatisfied for him with this his just and natural part of praise, and by way of doing him right must needs rise up to glorify him for imagination, of which he had little, and harmony, of which he had none. Even when supporting himself as in "Manfred" on the wings of other poets, he cannot fly as straight or sing as true as they. It is not the mere fluid melody of dulcet and facile verse that is wanting to him; that he might want and be none the worse for want of it; it is the inner sense of harmony which cannot but speak in music, the innate and spiritual instinct of sweetness and fitness and exaltation which cannot but express itself in height and perfection of song. This divine concord is never infringed or violated in the stormiest symphonies of passion or imagination by any one of the supreme and sovereign poets: by Æschylus or Shakespeare, in the tempest and agony of Prometheus or of Lear, it is no less surely and naturally preserved than by Sophocles or by Milton in the serener departure of Œdipus or the more temperate lament of Samson. In a free country Mr. Austin or any other citizen may of course take leave to set Byron beside Shelley or above him, as Byron himself had leave to set Pope beside or above Shakespeare and Milton; there is no harm done in either case even to Pope or Byron, and assuredly there is no harm done to the greater poets. The one thing memorable in the matter is the confidence with which men who have absolutely no sense whatever of verbal music will pronounce judgment on the subtlest questions relating to that form of art. A man whose ear is conscious of no difference between Offenbach and Beethoven does not usually stand up as a judge of instrumental music; but there is no ear so hirsute or so hard, so pointed or so long, that its wearer will not feel himself qualified to pass sentence on the musical rank of any poet's verse, the relative range and value of his metrical power or skill. If one man says for instance that Shelley outsang all rivals while Byron could not properly sing at all, and another man in reply is good enough to inform him that what he meant to say and should have said was that Byron could not shriek in falsetto like Shelley and himself, the one betweenwhiles and the other at all times, what answer or appeal is possible? The decision must be left to each man's own sense of hearing, or to his estimate of the respective worth of the two opinions given. I have always thought it somewhat hasty on the part of Sir Hugh Evans to condemn as " affectations " that phrase of Pistol's—" He hears with ears;" to hear with ears is a gift by no means given to every man that wears them. Our own meanwhile are still plagued with the cackle of such judges on all points of art as those to whom Molière addressed himself in vain—' qui blâment et louent tout à contre-sens, prennent par où ils peuvent les termes de l'art qu'ils attrapent, et ne manquent jamais de les estropier et de les mettre hors de place. Hé! morbleu! monsieurs, taisez-vous. *Quand Dieu ne vous a pas donné la connais-*

sance d'une chose, n'apprêtez point à rire à ceux qui vous entendent parler ; et songez qu'en ne disant mot on croira peut-être que vous êtes d'habiles gens." Such another critic as Mr. Austin is Herr Elze, the German biographer, who has been sent among us after many days to inform our native ignorance that Byron was the greatest lyric poet of England. A few more such examples should have been vouchsafed us of "things not generally known ;" such as these for instance : that our greatest dramatic poet was Dr. Johnson, our greatest comic poet was Sir Isaac Newton, our best amatory poet was Lord Bacon, our best religious poet was Lord Rochester, our best narrative poet was Joseph Addison, and our greatest epic poet was Tom Moore. Add to these the facts that Shakespeare's fame rests on his invention of gunpowder, and Milton's on his discovery of vaccination, and the student thus prepared and primed with useful knowledge will in time be qualified to match our instructor himself for accurate science of English literature, biographical or critical. It is a truth neither more nor less disputable than these that Byron was a great lyric poet ; if the statements proposed above be true, then that also is true ; if they be not, it also is not. He could no more have written a thoroughly good and perfect lyric, great or small, after the fashion of Hugo or after the fashion of Tennyson, than he could have written a page of Hamlet or of Paradise Lost. Even in the "Isles of Greece," excellent as the poem is throughout for eloquence and force, he stumbles into epigram or subsides into reflection with untimely lapse of rhetoric and unseemly change of note. The stanza on Miltiades is an almost vulgar instance of oratorical trick—" a very palpable hit" it might be on a platform, but it is a very palpable flaw in a lyric. Will it again be objected that such dissection as this of a poem is but a paltry and injurious form of criticism? Doubtless it is; but the test of true and great poetry is just this; that it will endure, if need be, such a process of analysis or anatomy; that thus tried as in the fire and decomposed as in a crucible it comes out after all renewed and reattested in perfection of all its parts, in solid and flawless unity, whole and indissoluble. Scarcely one or two of all Byron's poems will stand any such test for a moment: and his enemies, it must again be explained, are those eyeless and earless panegyrists who will not let us overlook this infirmity. It is to Byron and not to Tennyson that Mr. Austin has proved himself an enemy; the enemies of Tennyson are critics of another class: they are those of his own household. They are not the men who bring against the sweetest and the noblest examples of his lyric work their charges of pettiness or tameness, contraction or inadequacy; who taste a savour of corruption in "The Sisters" or a savour of effeminacy in "Boadicea." They are the men who couple "In Memoriam" with the Psalms of David as a work akin to these in scope and in effect; who compare the dramatic skill and subtle power to sound the depths of the human spirit displayed in "Maud" with the like display of these gifts in Hamlet and Othello. They are the men who would set his ode on the death of Wellington above Shelley's lines on the death of Napoleon, his "Charge of the Light Brigade" beside Campbell's "Battle of the Baltic" or Drayton's "Battle of Agincourt," the very poem whose model it follows afar off with such halting and unequal steps. They are the men who find in his collection of Arthurian idyls,— the Morte d'Albert as it might perhaps be more properly called, after the princely type to which (as he tells us with just pride) the poet has been fortunate enough to make his central figure so successfully conform,—an epic poem of profound and exalted morality. Upon this moral question I shall take leave to intercalate a few words. It does not appear to me that on the whole I need stand in fear of misapprehension or misrepresentation on one charge at least—that of envious or grudging reluctance to applaud the giver of any good gift for which all receivers should be glad to return thanks. I am not aware—but it is possible that this too may be an instance of a man's blindness to his own defects—of having by any overt or covert demonstration of so vile a spirit exposed my name to be classed with the names, whether forged or genuine, of the rancorous and reptile crew of poeticules who decompose into criticasters; I do not remember to have ever as yet been driven by despair or hunger or malevolence to take up the trade of throwing dirt in the dark; nor am I conscious, at sight of my superiors, of an instant impulse to revile them. My first instinct, in such a case, is not the instinct of backbiting; I have even felt at such times some moderate sense of delight and admiration, and some slight pleasure in the attempt to express it loyally by such modest thanksgiving as I might. I hold myself therefore free to say what I think on this matter without fear of being taxed with the motives of a currish malignant. It seems to me that the moral tone of the Arthurian story has been on the whole lowered and degraded by Mr. Tennyson's mode of treatment. Wishing to make his central figure the noble and perfect symbol of an ideal man, he has removed not merely the excuse but the explanation of the fatal and tragic loves of Launcelot and Guenevere. The hinge of the whole legend of the Round Table, from its first glory to its final fall, is the incestuous birth of Mordred from the connexion of Arthur with his half-sister, unknowing and unknown; as surely as the hinge of the Oresteia from first to last is the sacrifice at Aulis. From the immolation of Iphigenia springs the wrath of Clytæmnestra, with all its train of evils ensuing; from the sin of Arthur's youth proceeds the ruin of his reign and realm through the falsehood of his wife, a wife unloving and unloved. Remove in either case the plea which leaves the heroine less sinned against indeed than sinning, but yet not too base for tragic compassion and interest, and there remains merely the presentation of a vulgar adulteress. From the background of the one story the ignoble figure of Ægisthus starts into the foreground, and we see in place of the terrible and patient mother, perilous and piteous as a lioness bereaved, the congenial harlot of a coward and traitor. A poet undertaking to rewrite the Agamemnon, who should open his poem with some scene of dalliance or conspiracy between Ægisthus and Clytæmnestra and proceed to make of their common household intrigue the mainspring of his plan, would not more depress the design and lower the keynote of the Æschylean drama, than Mr. Tennyson has lowered the note and deformed the outline of the Arthurian story, by reducing Arthur to the level of a wittol, Guenevere to the level of a woman of intrigue, and Launcelot to the level of a "co-respondent." Treated as he has treated it, the story is rather a case for the divorce-court than for poetry. At the utmost it might serve the recent censor of his countrymen, the champion of morals so dear to President Thiers and the virtuous journalist who draws a contrast in favour of his chastity between him and other French or English authors, for a new study of the worn and wearisome old topic of domestic intrigue; but such "camelias" should be left to blow in the common hotbeds of the lower kind of novelist. Adultery must be tragic and exceptional to afford stuff for art to work upon; and the debased preference of Mr. Tennyson's heroine for a lover so much beneath her noble and faithful husband is as mean an instance as any day can show in its newspaper reports of a common woman's common sin. In the old story, the king, with the doom denounced in the beginning by Merlin hanging over all his toils and triumphs as a tragic shadow, stands apart in no undignified patience to await the end in its own good time of all his work and glory, with no eye for the pain and passion of the woman who sits beside him as queen rather than as wife. Such a figure is not unfit for the centre of a tragic action; it is neither ignoble nor inconceivable; but the besotted blindness of Mr. Tennyson's "blameless king" to the treason of a woman who has had the first and last of his love and the whole devotion of his blameless life is nothing more or less than pitiful and ridi-

culous. All the studious care and exquisite
eloquence of the poet can throw no genuine halo
round the sprouting brows of a royal husband who
remains to the very last the one man in his kingdom
insensible of his disgrace. The unclean taunt of
the hateful Vivien is simply the expression in vile
language of an undeniable truth; such a man as
this king is indeed hardly "man at all;" either
fool or coward he must surely be. Thus it is that
by the very excision of what may have seemed in
his eyes a moral blemish Mr. Tennyson has
blemished the whole story; by the very exaltation
of his hero as something more than man he has
left him in the end something less. The keystone
of the whole building is removed, and in place of a
tragic house of song where even sin had all the
dignity and beauty that sin can retain, and without
which it can afford no fit material for tragedy, we
find an incongruous edifice of tradition and invention where even virtue is made to seem either
imbecile or vile. The story as it stood of old had
in it something almost of Hellenic dignity and
significance; in it as in the great Greek legends
we could trace from a seemingly small root of evil
the birth and growth of a calamitous fate, not
sent by mere malevolence of heaven, yet in its awful
weight and mystery of darkness apparently out of
all due retributive proportion to the careless sin or
folly of presumptuous weakness which first incurred

its infliction; so that by mere hasty resistance and return of violence for violence a noble man may unwittingly bring on himself and all his house the curse denounced on parricide, by mere casual indulgence of light love and passing wantonness a hero king may unknowingly bring on himself and all his kingdom the doom imposed on incest. This presence and imminence of Ate inevitable as invisible throughout the tragic course of action can alone confer on such a story the proper significance and the necessary dignity; without it the action would want meaning and the passion would want nobility; with it, we may hear in the high funereal homily which concludes as with dirge-music the great old book of Sir Thomas Mallory some echo not utterly unworthy of that supreme lament of wondering and wailing spirits—

$$\pi\hat{o}\iota\ \delta\hat{\eta}\tau\alpha\ \kappa\rho\alpha\nu\epsilon\hat{\iota},\ \pi\hat{o}\hat{\iota}\ \kappa\alpha\tau\alpha\lambda\acute{\eta}\xi\epsilon\iota$$
$$\mu\epsilon\tau\alpha\kappa\text{οι}\mu\iota\sigma\theta\grave{\epsilon}\nu\ \mu\acute{\epsilon}\nu\text{os}\ \ddot{\alpha}\tau\eta\text{s};$$

The fatal consequence or corollary of this original flaw in his scheme is that the modern poet has been obliged to degrade all the other figures of the legend in order to bring them into due harmony with the degraded figures of Arthur and Guenevere. The courteous and loyal Gawain of the old romancers, already deformed and maligned in the version of Mallory himself, is here a vulgar traitor; the benignant Lady of the Lake, foster-mother of

Launcelot, redeemer and comforter of Pelleas, becomes the very vilest figure in all that cycle of more or less symbolic agents and patients which Mr. Tennyson has set revolving round the figure of his central wittol. I certainly do not share the objection of the virtuous journalist to the presentation in art of an unchaste woman; but I certainly desire that the creature presented should retain some trace of human or if need be of devilish dignity. The Vivien of Mr. Tennyson's idyl seems to me, to speak frankly, about the most base and repulsive person ever set forth in serious literature. Her impurity is actually eclipsed by her incredible and incomparable vulgarity—("*O ay,*" *said Vivien, " that were likely too*"). She is such a sordid creature as plucks men passing by the sleeve. I am of course aware that this figure appears the very type and model of a beautiful and fearful temptress of the flesh, the very embodied and ennobled ideal of danger and desire, in the chaster eyes of the virtuous journalist who grows sick with horror and disgust at the license of other French and English writers; but I have yet to find the French or English contemporary poem containing a passage that can be matched against the loathsome dialogue in which Merlin and Vivien discuss the nightly transgressions against chastity, within doors and without, of the various knights of Arthur's court. I do not remember that any modern poet whose fame has been assailed on the score of sensual immorality—say for instance the author of "Mademoiselle de Maupin" or the author of the "Fleurs du Mal"—has ever devoted an elaborate poem to describing the erotic fluctuations and vacillations of a dotard under the moral and physical manipulation of a prostitute. The conversation of Vivien is exactly described in the poet's own phrase—it is "as the poached filth that floods the middle street." Nothing like it can be cited from the verse which embodies other poetic personations of unchaste women. From the Cleopatra of Shakespeare and the Dalilah of Milton to the Phraxanor of Wells, a figure worthy to be ranked not far in design below the highest of theirs, we may pass without fear of finding any such pollution. Those heroines of sin are evil, but noble in their evil way; it is the utterly ignoble quality of Vivien which makes her so unspeakably repulsive and unfit for artistic treatment. "Smiling saucily," she is simply a subject for the police-court. The "Femmes Damnees" of Baudelaire may be worthier of hell-fire than a common harlot like this, but that side of their passion which would render them amenable to the notice of the nearest station is not what is kept before us throughout that condemned poem; it is an infinite perverse refinement, an infinite reverse aspiration, "the end of which things is death;" and from the barren places of unsexed desire the tragic lyrist points them at last along their downward way to the land of sleepless winds and scourging storms, where the shadows of things perverted shall toss and turn for ever in a Dantesque cycle and agony of changeless change; a lyric close of bitter tempest and deep wide music of lost souls, not inaptly described by M. Asselineau as a "fulgurant" harmony after the fashion of Beethoven. The slight sketch in eight lines of Matha in "Ratbert" resumes all the imaginable horror and loveliness of a wicked and beautiful woman; but Hugo does not make her open her lips to let out the foul talk or the "saucy" smile of the common street. "La blonde fauve," all but naked among the piled-up roses, with feet dabbled in blood, and the laughter of hell itself on her rosered mouth, is as horrible as any proper object of art can be; but she is not vile and intolerable as Vivien. I do not fear or hesitate to say on this occasion what I think and have always thought on this matter; for I trust to have shown before now that the poet in the sunshine of whose noble genius the men of my generation grew up and took delight has no more ardent or more loyal admirer than myself among the herd of imitative parasites and thievish satellites who grovel at his heels; that I need feel no apprehension of being placed "in the rank of verminous fellows" who let themselves out to lie for hatred or for hire—"qui quæstum non corporis sed animi sui faciunt," as Major Dalgetty might have defined them. Among these obscene vermin I do not hold myself liable to be classed; though I may be unworthy to express, however capable of feeling, the same abhorrence as the Quarterly reviewer of "Vivien" for the exhibition of the libidinous infirmity of unvenerable age. But these are not the grounds on which Mr. Austin objects to the ethical tendency of Mr. Tennyson's poetry. His complaint against all those of his countrymen who spend their time in writing verse is that their verse is devoted to the worship of "woman, woman, woman, woman." He "hardly likes to own sex with" a man who devotes his life to the love of a woman, and is ready to lay down his life and to sacrifice his soul for the chance of preserving her reputation. It is probable that the reluctance would be cordially reciprocated. A writer about as much beneath Mr. Austin as Mr. Austin is beneath the main objects of his attack has charged certain poetry of the present day with constant and distasteful recurrence of devotion to "some person of the other sex." It is at least significant that this person should have come forward, for once under his own name, to vindicate the moral worth of Petronius Arbiter; a writer, I believe, whose especial weakness (as exhibited in the characters of his book) was not a "hankering" after persons "of the other sex." It is as well to remember where we may be when we find ourselves in the company of these anti-sexual moralists.

Effeminate therefore I suppose the modern poetry of England must be content to remain; but there is a poet alive of now acknowledged eminence, not hitherto assailed on this hand, about whom the masked or barefaced critics of the minute are not by any means of one mind—if mind we are to call the organ which forms and produces their opinions. To me it seems that the truth for good and evil has never yet been spoken about Walt Whitman. There are in him two distinct men of most inharmonious kinds; a poet and a formalist. Of the poet I have before now done the best I could to express, whether in verse or prose, my ardent and sympathetic admiration. Of the formalist I shall here say what I think; showing why (for example) I cannot for my own part share in full the fiery partisanship of such thoughtful and eloquent disciples as Mr. Rossetti and Dr. Burroughs. It is from no love of foolish paradox that I have chosen the word "formalist" to express my sense of the radical fault in the noble genius of Whitman. For truly no scholar and servant of the past, reared on academic tradition under the wing of old-world culture, was ever more closely bound in with his own theories, more rigidly regulated by his own formularies, than this poet of new life and limitless democracy. Not

Pope, not Boileau, was more fatally a formalist
than Whitman; only Whitman is a poet of a
greater nature than they. It is simply that these
undigested formulas which choke by fits the free
passage of his genius are to us less familiar than
theirs; less real or less evident they are not.
Throughout his great book, now of late so nobly
completed, you can always tell at first hearing
whether it be the poet who speaks or the formalist.
Sometimes in the course of two lines the note is
changed, either by the collapse of the poet's voice
into the tuneless twang of the formalist, or by the
sudden break and rise of released music from the
formalist's droning note into the clear sincere
harmonies of the poet. Sometimes for one whole
division of the work either the formalist intones
throughout as to order, or the poet sings high and
true and strong without default from end to end.
It is of no matter whatever, though both disciples
and detractors appear to assume that it must be at
least in each other's eyes, whether the subject
treated be conventionally high or low, pleasant
or unpleasant. At once and without fail you
can hear whether the utterance of the subject be
right or wrong; this is the one thing needful; but
then this one thing is needful indeed. Disciples
and detractors alike seem to assume that if you
object to certain work of Whitman's it must be
because you object to his choice of topic and

would object equally to any man's choice or treatment of it ; if you approve, it must be that you approve of the choice of topic and would approve equally of any poem that should start for the same end and run on the same lines. It is not so in the least. Let a man come forward as does Whitman with prelude of promise that he is about to sing and celebrate certain things, fair or foul, great or small, these being as good stuff for song and celebration as other things, we wait, admitting that, to hear if he will indeed celebrate and sing them. If he does, and does it well and duly, there is an end ; *solvitur ambulando ;* the matter is settled once for all by the invaluable and indispensable proof of the pudding. Now whenever the pure poet in Whitman speaks, it is settled by that proof in his favour ; whenever the mere theorist in him speaks, it is settled by the same proof against him. What comes forth out of the abundance of his heart rises at once from that high heart to the lips on which its thoughts take fire, and the music which rolls from them rings true as fine gold and perfect ; what comes forth by the dictation of doctrinal theory serves only to twist aside his hand and make the written notes run foolishly awry. What he says is well said when he speaks as of himself and because he cannot choose but speak ; whether he speak of a small bird's loss or a great man's death, of a nation rising for battle or a child going forth in the morning. What he says is not well said when he speaks not as though he must but as though he ought; as though it behoved one who would be the poet of American democracy to do this thing or to be that thing if the duties of that office were to be properly fulfilled, the tenets of that religion worthily delivered. Never before was high poetry so puddled and adulterated with mere doctrine in its crudest form. Never was there less assimilation of the lower dogmatic with the higher prophetic element. It so happens that the present writer (*si quid id est*) is, as far as he knows, entirely at one with Whitman on general matters not less than on political; if there be in Whitman's works any opinion expressed on outward and social or inward and spiritual subjects which would clash or contend with his own, or with which he would feel his own to be incapable of concord or sympathy, he has yet to find the passage in which that opinion is embodied. To him the views of life and of death set forth by Whitman appear thoroughly acceptable and noble, perfectly credible and sane. It is certainly therefore from no prejudice against the doctrines delivered that he objects in any case to the delivery of them. What he objects—to take two small instances—is that it is one thing to sing the song of all trades, and quite another thing to tumble down together the names of all possible crafts and implements in one unsorted heap; to sing the song of all countries is not simply to fling out on the page at random in one howling mass the titles of all divisions of the earth, and so leave them. At this rate, to sing the song of the language it should suffice to bellow out backwards and forwards the twenty-four letters of the alphabet. And this folly is deliberately done by a great writer, and ingeniously defended by able writers, alike in good faith, and alike in blind bondage to mere dogmatic theory, to the mere formation of foregone opinion. They cannot see that formalism need not by any means be identical with tradition : they cannot see that because theories of the present are not inherited they do not on that account become more proper than were theories of the past to suffice of themselves for poetic or prophetic speech. Whether you have to deliver an old or a brand-new creed, alike in either case you must first insure that it be delivered well; for in neither will it suffice you to deliver it simply in good faith and good intent. The poet of democracy must sing all things alike? let him sing them then, whether in rhyme or not is no matter,*

---

* In Dr. Burroughs' excellent little book there is a fault common to almost all champions of his great friend ; they will treat Whitman as " Athanasius contra mundum :" they will assume that if he be right all other poets must be wrong ; and if this intimation were confined to America there might but in rhythm he must needs sing them. What is true of all poets is among them all most markedly true of Whitman, that his manner and his matter grow together; that where you catch a note of discord there you will find something wrong inly, the natural source of that outer wrongdoing;

---

be some plausible reason to admit it; but if we pass beyond and have to choose between Whitman and the world, we must regretfully drop the "Leaves of Grass" and retain at least for example the " Légende des Siècles." As to this matter of rhythm and rhyme, prose and verse, I find in this little essay some things which out of pure regard and sympathy I could wish away, and consigned to the more congenial page of some tenth-rate poeticule worn out with failure after failure, and now squat in his hole like the tailless fox he is, curled up to snarl and whimper beneath the inaccessible vine of song. Let me suggest that it may *not* be observed in the grand literary relics of nations that their best poetry has always, or has ever, adopted essentially the prose form, preserving interior rhythm only. I do not "ask dulcet rhymes from" Whitman; I far prefer his rhythms to any merely "dulcet metres;" I would have him in nowise other than he is; but I certainly do not wish to see his form or style reproduced at second-hand by a school of disciples with less deep and exalted sense of rhythm. As to rhyme, there is some rhymed verse that holds more music, carries more weight, flies higher and wider in equal scope of sense and sound, than all but the highest human speech has ever done; and would have done no more, as no verse has done more, had it been unrhymed; witness the song of the Earth from Shelley's "Prometheus Unbound." Do as well without rhyme if you can, or do as well with rhyme, it is of no moment whatever; a thing not noticeable or perceptible except by pedants and sciolists; in either case your triumph will be equal. In a precious and memorable excerpt given wherever you catch a note of good music you will surely find that it came whence only it could come, from some true root of music in the thought or thing spoken. There never was and will never be a poet who had verbal harmony and nothing else; if there was in him no inner depth or strength or truth, then that which men took for music in his mere speech was no such thing as music.

By far the finest and truest thing yet said of Walt Whitman has been said by himself, and said worthily of a great man. "I perceive in clear moments," he said to his friend Dr. Burroughs, "that my work is not the accomplishment of perfections, but destined, I hope, always to arouse an unquenchable feeling and ardour for them." A hope, surely, as well grounded as it is noble.

---

by Dr. Burroughs from some article in the *North American Review*, the writer, a German by his name, after much gabble against prosody, observes with triumph as a final instance of the progress of language that "*the spiritualizing and enfranchising influence* of Christianity transformed Greek into an accentuated language." The present poets of Greece, I presume, know better than to waste their genius on the same ridiculous elaborations of corresponsive metre which occupied the pagan and benighted intellects of Æschylus and Pindar. I have heard before now of many deliverances wrought by Christianity; but I had never yet perceived that among the most remarkable of these—"an outward and visible sign of an inward and spiritual grace"—was to be reckoned the transformation of the language spoken under Pericles into the language spoken under King Otho and King George.

But it is in those parts of his work which most arouse this feeling and this ardour that we find him nearest that accomplishment. At such times his speech has a majestic harmony which hurts us by no imperfection; his music then is absolutely great and good. It is when he is thinking of his part, of the duties and properties of a representative poet, an official democrat, that the strength forsakes his hand and the music ceases at his lips. It is then that he sets himself to define what books, and to what purpose, the scriptural code of democracy must accept and reject;.to determine, Pope himself and council in one, what shall be the canons and articles of the church, which except a democrat do keep whole and undefiled, without doubt he shall perish everlastingly. With more than Athanasian assurance, with more than Calvinistic rigour, it is then that he pronounces what things are democratic and of good report, what things are feudal and of evil report, in all past literature of the world. There is much in these canonical decrees that is consonant with truth and reason; there is not a little that is simply the babbling of a preacher made drunk with his own doctrine. For instance, we find that "the Democratic requirements" substantially and curiously fulfilled in the best Spanish literature are not only not fulfilled in the best English literature, but are insulted in every page. After this it appears to us that in common consistency the best remaining type of actual democracy in Europe here must be sought among French or Austrian Legitimists, if not on some imperial Russian or German throne. But Shakespeare is not only "the tally of Feudalism," he is "incarnated, uncompromising Feudalism in literature." Now Shakespeare has doubtless done work which is purely aristocratic in tone. The supreme embodiment in poetic form of the aristocratic idea is "Coriolanus." I cannot at all accept the very good special pleading of M. François-Victor Hugo against this the natural view of that great tragedy. Whether we like it or not, the fact seems to me undeniable that Shakespeare has here used all his art and might to subdue the many to the one, to degrade the figure of the people, to enhance and exalt the figure of the people's enemy. Even here, though, he has not done as in Whitman's view he does always; he has not left without shades the radiant figure, he has not left the sombre figure without lights; there are blemishes here and there on the towering glory of Coriolanus, redeeming points now and then in the grovelling ignominy of the commons. But what if there were none? Is this play the keynote of Shakespeare's mind, the keystone of his work? If the word Democracy mean anything—and to Whitman it means much—beyond the mere profession of a certain creed, the mere iteration of a certain shibboleth; if it signify first the cyclic life and truth of equal and various humanity, and secondly the form of principles and relations, the code of duties and of rights, by which alone adult society can walk straight; surely in the first and greatest sense there has never been and never can be a book so infinitely democratic as the Plays of Shakespeare.

These among others are reasons why I think it foolish to talk of Whitman as the probable founder of a future school of poetry unlike any other in matter as in style. He has many of the qualities of a reformer; he has perhaps none of the qualities of a founder. For one thing, he is far too didactic to be typical; the prophet in him too frequently subsides into the lecturer. He is not one of the everlasting models; but as an original and individual poet, it is at his best hardly possible to overrate him; as an informing and reforming element, it is absolutely impossible. Never did a country need more than America such an influence as his. We may understand and even approve his reproachful and scornful fear of the overweening " British element " when we see what it has hitherto signified in the literature of his country. Once as yet, and once only, has there sounded out of it all one pure note of original song—worth singing, and echoed from the singing of no other man; a note of song neither wide nor deep, but utterly true, rich, clear, and native to the singer ; the short exquisite music, subtle and simple and sombre and sweet, of Edgar Poe. All the rest that is not of mocking-birds is of corncrakes, varied but at best for an instant by some scant-winded twitter of linnet or of wren.

We have been looking up too long from the microscope ; it is time to look in again and take note of the subject. We find indeed one American name on which our weekly critics cluster in swarms of praise ; one poet whom they who agree in nothing else but hate agree to love and laud as king of American verse ; who has sung, they tell us, a song at last truly national and truly noble. The singer is Mr. Lowell ; but the song is none of the Biglow Papers, where the humours could not but tickle while the discords made us wince ; we laughed, with ears yet flayed and teeth still on edge. The song so preferable to any "Drum-Tap" of Whitman's was a Thanksgiving Ode of wooden verse sawn into unequal planks and tagged incongruously with tuneless bells of rhyme torn from the author's late professional cap. It was modelled on the chaotic songs of ceremony done to order on state occasions by our laureates of the Restoration and Revolution ; preferable in this alone, that the modern author had the grace not to call it Pindaric : which in the sense of Whitehall, not of Thebes, it was ; being cut into verses uneven, misshapen, irregular, and irresponsive. As a speech it might have passed muster on the platform ; as a song it gave out no sound but such as of the platform's wood. Nor indeed could it; for while it had something of thought and more of eloquence, there was within it no breath or pulse of the thing called poetry. This gracious chant among others has been much belauded—incomparably beyond any praise given in any such quarter to Whitman's deathless hymn of death—by a writer on poetry whom Mr. Austin has reviled with as much acrimony as if he were instead a poet ; calling his poor fellow-critic " an ignorant and presumptuous scribbler, wholly unentitled to give an opinion on poetry at all." Far be it from me this time to dispute the perfect justice of the verdict; but I had some hope till now that there might be truth in the proverb, " Hawks do not pyke out hawks' een." It is painful for the naturalist to be compelled to register in his note-book the fact that there is none. It is sad that the hymnologist, to whom this fact may be yet unknown, should be obliged, after citing the peaceful example of the aviary, to reiterate the lesson that 'tis a shameful sight when critics of one progeny fall out and chide and fight.*

---

* I cannot help calling just now to mind an epigram—very rude, after the fashion of the time, but here certainly not impertinent but pertinent—cited by Boswell on a quarrel between two " beaux ;" the second stanza runs thus, with

Really they should remember that their office is to instruct; and if so, surely not by precept alone. If the monitors of the poetic school go together by the ears in this way in sight of all forms at once, what can be expected of those whom they were appointed (though God only knows by whom) to direct and correct at need? The dirtiest little sneak on the dunce's seat may be encouraged to play some blackguard's trick on better boys behind their backs, and so oblige some one who had no thought of bullying or of noticing such a cur to kick him out into the yard and cleanse the old school of scandalous rubbish. And what may not one of the head-masters (there are more than one in this school), at their next quarterly visitation, say to such a couple of monitors as this?

> "Their little hands were never made
> To tear each other's eyes."

Their little hands—can it be necessary to remind them?—were made to throw dirt and stones with impunity at passers-by of a different kind. This is their usual business, and they do it with a will; though (to drop metaphor for awhile) we may con-

---

one word altered of necessity, as that quarrel was not on poetry but on religion:—

> "Peace, coxcombs, peace! and both agree;
> A., kiss thy empty brother;
> The Muses love a foe like thee,
> But dread a friend like t'other."

cede that English reviewers—and among them the reviewer of the " Spectator "—have not always been unready to do accurate justice to the genuine worth of new American writers; among much poor patchwork of comic and serious stuff, which shared their welcome and diminished its worth, they have yet found some fit word of praise for the true pathos of Bret Harte, the true passion of Joaquin Miller. But the men really and naturally dear to them are the literators of Boston; truly, and in no good sense, the school of New England —Britannia pejor; a land of dissonant reverberations and distorted reflections from our own.* This preference for the province of reflex poets and

---

* Not that the British worshipper gets much tolerance for his countrymen in return. In an eloquent essay on the insolence of Englishmen towards Americans, for which doubtless there are but too good grounds, Mr. Lowell shows himself as sore as a whipped cutpurse of the days " ere carts had lost their tails " under the vulgar imputation of vulgarity. It is doubtless a very gross charge, and one often flung at Americans by English lackeys and bullies of the vulgarest order. Is there ever any ground for it discernible in the dainty culture of overbred letters which, as we hear, distinguishes New England ? I remember to have read a passage from certain notes of travel in Italy published by an eminent and eloquent writer—that I could but remember his name and grace my page with it !—who after some just remarks on Byron's absurd and famous description of a waterfall, proceeds to observe that Milton was the only poet who ever made real poetry out of a cataract—" AND THAT WAS IN HIS EYE."

echoing philosophers came to a climax of expression in the transcendant remark that Mr. Lowell had in one critical essay so taken Mr. Carlyle to pieces, that it would seem impossible ever to put him together again. Under the stroke of that recollected sentence, the staggered spirit of a sane man who desires to retain his sanity can but pause and reflect on what Mr. Ruskin, if I rightly remember, has somewhere said, that ever since Mr. Carlyle began to write you can tell by the reflex action of his genius the nobler from the ignobler of his contemporaries; as ever having won the most of reverence and praise from the most honourable among these, and (what is perhaps as sure a warrant of sovereign worth) from the most despicable among them the most of abhorrence and abuse.

A notable example of this latter sort was not long since (in his "Fors Clavigera") selected and chastised by Mr. Ruskin himself with a few strokes of such a lash as might thenceforward, one would think, have secured silence at least, if neither penitence nor shame, on the part of the offender. This person, whose abuse of Mr. Carlyle he justly describes as matchless "in its platitudinous obliquity," was cited by the name of one Buchanan—

ὅστις ποτ' ἐστὶν, εἰ τόδ' αὐ-
τῷ φίλον κεκλημένῳ—

but whether by his right name or another, who

shall say? for the god of song himself had not more names or addresses. Now yachting among the Scottish (not English) Hebrides; now wrestling with fleshly sin (like his countryman Holy Willie) in "a great city of civilization;" now absorbed in studious emulation of the Persæ of Æschylus or the "enormously fine" work of "the tremendous creature" Dante;* now descending from the familiar heights of men whose praise he knows so well how to sing, for the not less noble purpose of crushing a school of poetic sensualists whose works are "wearing to the brain;" now "walking down the streets" and watching "harlots stare from the shop-windows," while "in the broad day a dozen hands offer him indecent prints;" now "beguiling many an hour, when snug at anchor in some lovely Highland loch, with the inimitable, yet questionable, pictures of Parisian life left by Paul de Kock;" landsman and seaman, Londoner and Scotchman, Delian and Patarene Buchanan. How should one address him?

"Matutine pater, seu Jane libentiùs audis?"

As Janus rather, one would think, being so in all

---

* Lest it should seem impossible that these and the like could be the actual expressions of any articulate creature, I have invariably in such a context marked as quotations only the exact words of this unutterable author, either as I find them cited by others or as they fall under my own eye in glancing among his essays. More trouble than this I am not disposed to take with him.

men's sight a natural son of the double-faced divinity. Yet it might be well for the son of Janus if he had read and remembered in time the inscription on the statue of another divine person, before taking his name in vain as a word wherewith to revile men born in the ordinary way of the flesh:—

> "Youngsters ! who write false names, and slink behind
> The honest garden-god to hide yourselves,
> Beware !"

In vain would I try to play the part of a prologuizer before this latest rival of the Hellenic dramatists, who sings from the height of "mystic realism," not with notes echoed from a Grecian strain, but as a Greek poet himself might have sung, in "massive grandeur of style," of a great contemporary event. He alone is fit, in Euripidean fashion, to prologuize for himself.

> Πολλὸς μὲν ἐν γραφαῖσι κοὐκ ἀνώνυμος
> ψεύστης κέκλημαι Σκότιος, * ἄστεως τ' ἔσω,
> ὅσοι τε πόντου τερμόνων τ' Ἀτλαντικῶν
> ναίουσιν ἔξω σκάφεσι νησιωτικοῖς,
> τοὺς μὲν τρέφοντας θώψ ἀπὸ γλώσσης σέβω,
> ὅσοι δ' ἀποπτύουσί μ' ἐμπίπτω λαθών.†

He has often written, it seems, under false or

---

* For the occasions on which the word σκότιος is to be spelt with a capital Σ, the student should consult the last-century glossaries of Lauder and Macpherson.

† There are other readings of the two last lines :
τοὺς δεσπότας μὲν δουλιᾷ σαίνω φρενί,
ὅσοι δὲ μ'ἀγνοοῦσιν (Cod. Var. ὅσοισι δ' εἰμ' ἄγνωτος) κ. τ. λ.

assumed names; always doubtless "with the best of all motives," that which induced his friends in his absence to alter an article abusive of his betters and suppress the name which would otherwise have signed it, that of saving the writer from persecution and letting his charges stand on their own merits; and this simple and very natural precaution has singularly enough exposed his fair fame to "the inventions of cowards"—a form of attack naturally intolerable though contemptible to this polyonymous moralist. He was not used to it; in the cradle where his genius had been hatched he could remember no taint of such nastiness. Other friends than such had fostered into maturity the genius that now lightens far and wide the fields of poetry and criticism. All things must have their beginnings; and there were those who watched with prophetic hope the beginnings of Mr. Buchanan; who tended the rosy and lisping infancy of his genius with a care for its comfort and cleanliness not unworthy the nurse of Orestes; and took indeed much the same pains to keep it sweet and neat under the eye and nose of the public as those on which the good woman dwelt with such pathetic minuteness of recollection in after years. The babe may not always have been discreet;

νέα δὲ νηδὺς αὐτάρκης τέκνων·

and there were others who found its swaddling

clothes not invariably in such condition as to dispense with the services of the "fuller;"

γναφεὺς τροφεύς τε ταὐτὸν εἰχέτην τέλος.

In effect there were those who found the woes and devotions of Doll Tearsheet or Nell Nameless as set forth in the lyric verse of Mr. Buchanan calculated rather to turn the stomach than to melt the heart. But in spite of these exceptional tastes the nursing journals, it should seem, abated no jot of heart or hope for their nursling.

> " Petit poisson deviendra grand
> Pourvu que Dieu lui prête vie."

Petit bonhomme will not, it appears. The tadpole poet will never grow into anything bigger than a frog; not though in that stage of development he should puff and blow himself till he bursts with windy adulation at the heels of the laurelled ox.

When some time since a passing notice was bestowed by writers of another sort on Mr. Buchanan's dramatic performance in the part of Thomas Maitland, it was observed with very just indignation by a literary ally that Mr. Rossetti was not ashamed to avow in the face of heaven and the press his utter ignorance of the writings of that poet—or perhaps we should say of those poets. The loss was too certainly his own. It is no light thing for a man who has any interest in the poetic production of his time to be ignorant of works which have won from the critic, who of all others must be most competent to speak on the subject with the authority of the most intimate acquaintance, such eloquence of praise as has deservedly been lavished on Mr. Buchanan. A living critic of no less note in the world of letters than himself has drawn public attention to the deep and delicate beauties of his work; to "the intense loving tenderness of the coarse woman Nell towards her brutal paramour, the exquisite delicacy and fine spiritual vision of the old village schoolmaster," &c. &c. This pathetic tribute to the poet Buchanan was paid by no less a person than Buchanan the critic. Its effect is heightened by comparison with the just but rigid severity of that writer's verdict on other men—on the "gross" work of Shakespeare, the "brutal" work of Carlyle, the "sickening and peculiar" work of Thackeray, the "wooden-headed," "hectic," and "hysterical" qualities which are severally notable and condemnable in the work of Landor, of Keats, and of Shelley. In like manner his condemnation of contemporary impurities is thrown into fuller relief by his tribute to the moral sincerity of Petronius and the "singular purity" of Ben Jonson. For once I have the honour and pleasure to agree with him; I find the "purity" of the author of "Bartholomew Fair" a very "singular" sort of purity indeed. There is however another play of that great writer's, which, though it might be commended by his well-wishers to the special study of Mr. Buchanan, I can hardly suppose to be the favourite work which has raised the old poet so high in his esteem. In this play Jonson has traced with his bitterest fidelity the career of a "gentleman parcel-poet," one Laberius Crispinus, whose life is spent in the struggle to make his way among his betters by a happy alternation and admixture of calumny with servility; one who will fasten himself uninvited on the acquaintance of a superior with fulsome and obtrusive ostentation of good-will; inflict upon his passive and reluctant victim the recitation of his verses in a public place; offer him friendship and alliance against all other poets, so as "to lift the best of them out of favour;" protest to him, "Do but taste me once, if I do know myself and my own virtues truly, thou wilt not make that esteem of Varius, or Virgil, or Tibullus, or any of 'em indeed, as now in thy ignorance thou dost; which I am content to forgive; I would fain see which of these could pen more verses in a day or with more facility than I." After this, it need hardly be added that the dog returns to his vomit, and has in the end to be restrained by authority from venting "divers and sundry calumnies" against the victim aforesaid "or any other eminent man transcending him in merit, whom his envy shall find cause to work upon, either for that, or for keeping himself in better acquaintance, or enjoying better friends;"

and the play is aptly wound up by his public exposure and ignominious punishment. The title of this admirable comedy is "The Poetaster; or, His Arraignment;" and the prologue is spoken by Envy.

It is really to be regretted that the new fashion of self-criticism should never have been set till now. How much petty trouble, how many paltry wrangles and provocations, what endless warfare of the cranes and pigmies might have been prevented—and by how simple a remedy! How valuable would the applauding comments of other great poets on their own work have been to us for all time! All students of poetry must lament that it did not occur to Milton for example to express in public his admiration of "Paradise Lost." It might have helped to support the reputation of that poem against the severe sentence passed by Mr. Buchanan on its frequently flat and prosaic quality. And, like all truly great discoveries, this one looks so easy now we have it before us, that we cannot but wonder it was reserved for Mr. Buchanan to make: we cannot but feel it singular that Mr. Tennyson should never have thought fit to call our attention in person to the beauties of "Maud:" that Mr. Browning should never have come forward, "motley on back and pointing-pole in hand," to bid us remark the value of "The Ring and the Book;"

that Mr. Arnold should have left to others the task of praising his "Thyrsis" and "Empedocles." The last-named poet might otherwise have held his own even against the imputation of writing "mere prose" which now he shares with Milton: so sharp is the critical judgment, so high the critical standard, of the author of "The Book of Orm."

However, even in the face of the rebuke so deservedly incurred by the avowal of Mr. Rossetti's gross and deplorable ignorance of that and other great works from the same hand, I am bound in honesty to admit that my own studies in that line are hardly much less limited. I cannot profess to have read any book of Mr. Buchanan's; for aught I know, they may deserve all his praises; it is neither my business nor my desire to decide. But sundry of his contributions in verse and prose to various magazines and newspapers I have looked through or glanced over—not, I trust, without profit; not, I know, without amusement. From these casual sources I have gathered—as he who runs may gather—not a little information on no unimportant matters of critical and autobiographical interest. With the kindliest forethought, the most judicious care to anticipate the anxious researches of a late posterity, Mr. Buchanan has once and again poured out his personal confidences into the sympathetic bosom of the nursing journals.

He is resolved that his country shall not always have cause to complain how little she knows of her greatest sons. Time may have hidden from the eye of biography the facts of Shakespeare's life, as time has revealed to the eye of criticism the grossness of his works and the purity of his rival's; but none need fear that the next age will have to lament the absence of materials for a life of Buchanan. Not once or twice has he told in simple prose of his sorrows and aspirations, his struggles and his aims. He has told us what good man gave him in his need a cup of cold water, and what bad man accused him of sycophancy in the expression of his thanks. He has told us what advantage was taken of his tender age by heartless publishers, what construction was put upon his gushing gratitude by heartless reviewers. He has told us that he never can forget his first friends; he has shown us that he never can forget himself. He has told us that the versicles of one David Gray, a poor young poeticule of the same breed as his panegyrist (who however, it should in fairness be said, died without giving any sign of future distinction in the field of pseudonymous libel), will be read when the works of other contemporaries " have gone to the limbo of affettuosos." (May I suggest that the library edition of Mr. Buchanan's collected works should be furnished with a glossary for the use of students unskilled in the varieties of the Buchananese dialect? Justly contemptuous as he has shown himself of all foreign affectations of speech or style in an English writer, such a remarkable word in its apparent defiance of analogy as the one last quoted is not a little perplexing to their ignorance. I hardly think it can be Scotch; at least to a southern eye it bears no recognizable affinity to the language of Burns.) In like manner, if we may trust the evidence of Byron, did Porson prophesy of Southey that his epics would be read when Homer and Virgil were forgotten; and in like manner may the humblest of his contemporaries prophesy that Mr. Buchanan's idyls will be read by generations which have forgotten the idyls of Theocritus and of Landor, of Tennyson and of Chénier.

In that singularly interesting essay on "his own tentatives" from which we have already taken occasion to glean certain flowers of comparative criticism Mr. Buchanan remarks of this contemporary that he seems rather fond of throwing stones in his (Mr. Buchanan's) direction. This contemporary however is not in the habit of throwing stones; it is a pastime which he leaves to the smaller fry of the literary gutter. These it is sometimes not unamusing to watch as they dodge and shirk round the street-corner after the discharge of their popgun pellet, with the ready plea on their lips that it

was not this boy but that—not the good boy
Robert, for instance, but the rude boy Thomas.
But there is probably only one man living who
could imagine it worth his contemporary's while to
launch the smallest stone from his sling in such a
direction as that—who could conceive the very
idlest of marksmen to be capable of taking
aim unprovoked at so pitiful a target. Mr.
Buchanan and his nursing journals have informed
us that to his other laurels he is entitled to add
those of an accomplished sportsman. Surely
he must know that there are animals which
no one counts as game—which are classed under
quite another head than that. Their proper
designation it is needless here to repeat; it is
one that suffices to exempt them from the
honour and the danger common to creatures of a
higher kind. Of their natural history I did not
know enough till now to remark without surprise
that specimens of the race may be found which are
ambitious to be ranked among objects of sport.
For my part, as long as I am not suspected of any
inclination to join in the chase, such an one should
be welcome to lay that flattering unction to his
soul, and believe himself in secret one of the
nobler beasts of game; even though it were but a
weasel that would fain pass muster as a hart of
grice. It must no doubt be "very soothing" to Mr.
Buchanan's modesty to imagine himself the object

of such notice as he claims to have received; but
we may observe from how small a seed so large a
growth of self-esteem may shoot up:—

σμικροῦ γένοιτ' ἂν σπέρματος μέγας πύθμην·

from a slight passing mention of "idyls of the
gutter and the gibbet," in a passage referring to the
idyllic schools of our day, Mr. Buchanan has built
up this fabric of induction; he is led by even so
much notice as this to infer that his work must be
to the writer an object of especial attention, and
even (God save the mark!) of especial attack. He
is welcome to hug himself in that fond belief, and
fool himself to the top of his bent; but he will
hardly persuade any one else that to find his "neck-
verse" merely repulsive; to feel no responsive
vibration to "the intense loving tenderness" of his
street-walker, as she· neighs and brays over her
"gallows-carrion;" is the same thing as to deny the
infinite value, the incalculable significance, to a
great poet, of such matters as this luckless poeticule has here taken into his "hangman's
hands." Neither the work nor the workman
is to be judged by the casual preferences of social
convention. It is not more praiseworthy or more
pardonable to write bad verse about costermongers
and gaol-birds than to write bad verse about kings
and knights; nor (as would otherwise naturally be
the case) is it to be expected that because some
among the greatest of poets have been born among

the poorest of men, therefore the literature of a nation is to suffer joyfully an inundation or eruption of rubbish from all threshers, cobblers, and milkwomen who now, as in the age of Pope, of Johnson, or of Byron, may be stung to madness by the gadfly of poetic ambition. As in one rank we find for a single Byron a score of Roscommons, Mulgraves, and Winchilseas, so in another rank we find for a single Burns a score of Ducks, Bloomfields, and Yearsleys. And if it does not follow that a poet must be great if he be but of low birth, neither does it follow that a poem must be good if it be but written on a subject of low life. The sins and sorrows of all that suffer wrong, the oppressions that are done under the sun, the dark days and shining deeds of the poor whom society casts out and crushes down, are assuredly material for poetry of a most high order; for the heroic passion of Victor Hugos, for the angelic passion of Mrs. Brownings. Let another such arise to do such work as "Les Pauvres Gens" or the "Cry of the Children," and there will be no lack of response to that singing. But they who can only "grate on their scrannel-pipes of wretched straw" some pitiful "idyl" to milk the maudlin eyes of the nursing journals, must be content with such applause as their own; for in higher latitudes they will find none.

It is not my purpose in this little scientific excursion to remark further than may be necessary on the symptoms of a poetical sort which the skilful eye may discern in the immediate objects of examination. To play the critic of their idyllic or satirical verse is not an office to which my ambition can aspire. Nevertheless, in the process of research, it may be useful to take note of the casual secretions observable in a fine live specimen of the breed in which we are interested, as well as of its general properties; for thus we may be the better able to determine, if we find that worth while, its special and differential attributes. I have therefore given a first and last glance to the poetic excretions of the present subject. Even from such things as these there might be something to learn, if men would bring to a task so unpromising and uninviting the patient eye and humble spirit of·investigation by experiment. Such investigation would secure them against the common critical fallacy of assuming that a poem must be good because written on a subject, and it may be written with an aim, not unworthy of a better man than the writer; that a bad poem, for instance, on the life of our own day and the sorrows of our own people can only be condemned by those who would equally condemn a good poem on the same subject; who would admit nothing as fit matter for artistic handling, which was not of a more remote and ideal kind than this: a theory invaluable to all worthless and ambitious journeymen of verse, who, were it once admitted as a law, would have only the trouble left them of selecting the subject whereon to emit their superfluity of metrical matter. Akin to this is a fallacy more amiable if not less absurd; the exact converse of the old superstition that anything written "by a person of quality" must be precious and praiseworthy. The same unreasoning and valueless admiration is now poured out at the feet of almost any one who comes forward under the contrary plea, as a poet of the people; and men forget that by this promiscuous effusion of praise they betray as complete a disbelief in any real equality of natural rank as did those who fell down before their idols of the other class. Such critics seem bent on verifying the worn old jest of the Irish reformer: "Is not one man as good as another; ay, and a deal better too?" No one now writes or speaks as if he supposed that every man born in what is called the aristocratic class must needs and naturally, if he should make verses, take his place beside Shelley or Byron; the assumption would be felt on all hands as an impertinence rather than a compliment offered to that class; and how can it be other than an impertinence offered to a larger class to assume, or pretend to assume, that any one born in the opposite rank who may be put forward as a poet must naturally be the equal of Béranger or of Burns? Such an assumption is simply an inverted form of tuft-hunting; it implies at once the arrogant condescension of the patron to his parasite, and the lurking contempt of the parasite for his patron; not a beautiful or profitable combination of qualities.

A critic in the *Contemporary Review*, but neither Robert Maitland nor Thomas Buchanan, once took occasion to inquire with emphatic sarcasm, what did Shelley care, or what does another writer whom he did the honour to call the second Shelley—how undeservedly no one can be more conscious than the person so unduly exalted—care for the people, for the sufferings and the cause of the poor? To be accused of caring no more for the people than Shelley did may seem to some men much the same thing as to be accused of caring no more for France than Victor Hugo does, or for Italy than did one whose name I will not now bring into such a paper as this. But to some men, on the other hand, it may appear that this cruel charge will serve to explain the jealous acrimony with which the writer thus condemned and dismissed in such evil company "seems" incessantly and secretly to have assailed the fame of Mr. Buchanan—the rancorous malignity with which he must have long looked up from the hiding-place of a furtive obscurity towards the unapproachable heights, the unattainable honours, of the mountains climbed and the prizes grasped by the Poet of the Poor. It mattered little that his disguise was impenetrable to every other eye; that those nearest him had no suspicion of the villainous design which must ever have been at work in his brain, even when itself unconscious of itself; that his left hand knew not what his right hand was doing (as it most certainly did not) when it cast stones at the sweet lyrist of the slums; masked and cloaked, under the thickest muffler of anonymous or pseudonymous counterfeit, the stealthy and cowering felon stood revealed to the naked eye of honesty—stood detected, convicted, exposed to the frank and fearless gaze of Mr. Buchanan. Can a figure more pitiful or more shameful be conceived? The only atonement that can ever be made for such a rascally form of malevolence is that which is here offered in the way of confession and penance; the only excuse that can be advanced for such a viperous method of attack is that envy and hatred of his betters have ever been the natural signs and the inevitable appanages of a bad poet, whether he had studied in the fleshly or the skinny school. Remembering this, we can but too easily understand how Mr. Buchanan may have excited the general ill-will of his inferiors; we may deplore, but we cannot wonder, that the author of "Liz" and "Nell" should have aroused a sense of impotent envy in the author of "Jenny" and "Sister Helen;" it would not surprise though it could not but grieve us to hear that the author of "The

Earthly Paradise" was inwardly consumed by the canker of jealousy when he thought of the "Legends of Inverburn;" while with burning cheeks and downcast eyes it must be confessed that the author of "Atalanta in Calydon" may well be the prey of rancour yet more keen than theirs when he looks on the laurels that naturally prevent him from sleeping—the classic chaplets that crown the author of "Undertones."

It is but too well known that the three minor minstrels above named, who may perhaps be taken as collectively equivalent in station and intelligence to the single Buchanan, have long been banded together in a dark and unscrupulous league to decry all works and all reputations but their own. In the first and third persons of this unholy trinity the reptile passions of selfishness and envy have constantly broken out in every variety of ugliness; in the leprous eruption of naked insult, in the cancerous process of that rank and rotten malevolence which works its infectious way by hints and indications, in the nervous spasm of epileptic agony which convulses the whole frame of the soul at another's praise, and ends in a sort of moral tetanus at sight of another's triumph. That thus, and thus only, have their wretched spirits been affected by the spectacle of good and great things done by other men, the whole course of their artistic life and the whole tenor of their critical or illustrative work may be cited against them to bear witness. The least reference to the latter will suffice to show the narrow range and the insincere assumption of their hollow and self-centred sympathies, the poisonous bitterness and the rancorous meanness of their furtive and virulent antipathies. Thomas Maitland, in his character of the loyal detective, has also done the state of letters some service by exposing the shameless reciprocity of systematic applause kept up on all hands by this " mutual admiration society." Especial attention should be given to the candid and clear-sighted remarks of the critic on the "puffing" reviews of his accomplices by the senior member of the gang, and of the third party to this plot by both his colleagues in corruption and conspiracy. If any one outside their obscure and restricted circle of reciprocal intrigue and malignant secrecy has ever won from any of them the slightest dole of reluctant and grudging commendation, it has been easily traceable to the muddy source of self-interest or of sycophancy. To men of such long-established eminence and influence that it must evidently bring more of immediate profit to applaud them than to revile, there are writers who will ever be at hand to pour the nauseous libations of a parasite. Envy itself in such natures will change places on alternate days with self-interest; and a hand which the poor cur's tooth would otherwise be fain to bite, his tongue will then be fain to beslaver. More especially when there is a chance of discharging its natural venom in the very act of that servile caress ; when the obsequious lip finds a way to insinuate by flattery of one superior some stealthy calumny of another. "Ah, my lord and master," says the jackal to the lion (or for that matter to any other animal from whose charity or contempt it may hope for toleration and a stray bone or so now and then), "observe how all other living creatures belong but to some sub-leonine class,* some school of dependents and subordinates such as the poor slave who has now the honour to lick your foot !" This is a somewhat ignoble attitude on the poor slave's part, though excusable perhaps in a hungry four-footed brute ; but if any such biped as a minor poet were to play such a game as this of the jackal's, what word could we properly apply to him ? and what inference should we be justified in drawing as to the origin of his vicious antipathy to other names not less eminent than his chosen

---

* If we could imagine about 1820 some parasitic poeticule of the order of Kirke White classifying together Coleridge and Keats, Byron and Shelley, as members of "the sub-Wordsworthian school," we might hope to find an intellectual ancestor for Mr. Robert Buchanan ; but that hope is denied us ; we are reduced to believe that Mr. Buchanan must be autochthonous, or sprung perhaps from a cairngorm pebble cast behind him by the hand of some Scotch Deucalion.

patron's? Might we not imagine that some of the men at whose heels he now snaps instead of cringing have found it necessary before now to "spurn him like a cur out of their way"? It is of course possible that a man may honestly admire Mr. Tennyson who feels nothing but scorn and distaste for Mr. Carlyle or Mr. Thackeray; but if the latter feeling, expressed as it may be with barefaced and open-mouthed insolence, be as genuine and natural to him as the former, sprung from no petty grudge or privy spite, but reared in the normal soil or manured with the native compost of his mind,—the admiration of such an one is hardly a thing to be desired.

If however any one of that envious and currish triumvirate whom the open voice of honest criticism has already stigmatized should think in future of setting a trap for the illustrious object of their common malice, he will, it is to be hoped, take heed that his feet be not caught in his own snare. He will remember that the judgment of men now or hereafter on the work of an artist in any kind does not wholly depend on the evidence or the opinions of any Jack Alias or Tom Alibi who may sneak into court and out again when detected. He will not think to protect himself from the degradation of public exposure by the assumption of some such pseudonym as Joseph Surface or Seth Pecksniff. He will not feel that all is safe when he has assured the public that a review article alternating between covert praise of himself and overt abuse of his superiors was only through the merest inadvertence not issued in his own name; that it never would have appeared under the signature of Mr. Alias but that Mr. Alibi happened by the most untoward of accidents to be just then away " in his yacht" on a cruise among " the western Hebrides;" otherwise, and but for the blundering oversight of some unhappy publisher or editor, the passages which refer with more or less stealthy and suggestive insinuation of preference or of praise to the avowed publications of Mr. Alibi would have come before us with the warrant of that gentleman's honoured name. Credat Judæus Apella! but even the foolishest of our furtive triumvirate will hardly, I should imagine, expect that any son of circumcision or of uncircumcision would believe such a "legend" or give ear to such an "idyl" as that. Rather will he be inclined to meditate somewhat thus, after the fashion of the American poetess at Elijah Pogram's levee: " To be presented to a Maitland," he will reflect, " by a Buchanan, indeed, an impressive moment is it on what we call our feelings. But why we call them so, or why impressed they are, or if impressed they are at all, or if at all we are, or if there really is, oh gasping one! a Maitland or a Buchanan, or any active principle to which we give those titles, is a topic spirit-searching, light-abandoned, much too vast to enter on at this unlooked-for crisis." Or it may be he will call to mind an old couplet of some such fashion as this :—

> "A man of letters would Crispinus be ;
> He is a man of letters ; yes, of three."

How many names he may have on hand it might not be so easy to resolve: nor which of these, if any, may be genuine ; but for the three letters he need look no further than his Latin dictionary ; if such a reference be not something more than superfluous for a writer of "epiludes" who renders "domus exilis Plutonia" by "a Plutonian house of exiles:" a version not properly to be criticized in any "school" by simple application of goose-quill to paper.* The disciple on whom "the deep

---

* I am reminded here of another contemporary somewhat more notorious than this classic namesake and successor of George Buchanan, but like him a man of many and questionable names, who lately had occasion, while figuring on a more public stage than that of literature, to translate the words "Laus Deo semper" by "The laws of God for ever." It must evidently be from the same source that Mr. Buchanan and the Tichborne claimant have drawn their first and last draught of "the humanities." Fellow-students, whether at Stonyhurst or 'elsewhere, they ought certainly to have been. Can it be the rankling recollection of some boyish quarrel in which he came by the worst of it that keeps alive in the noble soul of Mr. Buchanan a dislike of "fleshly persons?" The result would be worthy of such a

delicious stream of the Latinity" of Petronius has made such an impression that he finds also a deep delicious morality in the pure and sincere pages of a book from which less pure-minded readers and writers less sincere than himself are compelled to turn away sick and silent with disgust after a second vain attempt to look it over—this loving student and satellite so ready to shift a trencher at the banquet of Trimalchio—has less of tolerance, we are scarcely surprised to find, for Æschylean Greece than for Neronian Rome. Among the imperfect and obsolete productions of the Greek stage he does indeed assign a marked pre-eminence

---

"fons et origo mali"—a phrase, I may add for the benefit of such scholars, which is not adequately ore xactly rendered by "the fount of original sin." Perhaps some day we may be gratified—but let us hope without any necessary intervention of lawyers—by some further discovery of the early associations which may have clustered around the promising boyhood of Thomas Maitland. Meantime it is a comfort to reflect that the assumption of a forged name for a dirty purpose does not always involve the theft of thousands, or the ruin of any reputation more valuable than that of a literary underling. May we not now also hope that Mr. Buchanan's fellow-scholar will be the next (in old-world phrase) to "oblige the reading public" with his views on ancient and modern literature? For such a work, whether undertaken in the calm of Newgate or the seclusion of the Hebrides, or any other haunt of lettered ease and leisure, he surely could not fail to find a publisher who in his turn would not fail to find him an *alibi* whenever necessary —whether eastward or westward of St. Kilda.

over all others to the Persæ. To the famous epitaph of Æschylus which tells only in four terse lines of his service as a soldier against the Persians, there should now be added a couplet in commemoration of the precedence granted to his play by a poet who would not stoop to imitate and a student who need not hesitate to pass sentence. Against this good opinion, however, we are bound to set on record the memorable expression of that deep and thoughtful contempt which a mind so enlightened and a soul so exalted must naturally feel for "the shallow and barbarous myth of Prometheus." Well may this incomparable critic, this unique and sovereign arbiter of thought and letters ancient and modern, remark with compassion and condemnation how inevitably a training in Grecian literature must tend to "emasculate" the student so trained: and well may we congratulate ourselves that no such process as robbed of all strength and manhood the intelligence of Milton has had power to impair the virility of Mr. Buchanan's robust and masculine genius. To that strong and severe figure we turn from the sexless and nerveless company of shrill-voiced singers who share with Milton the curse of enforced effeminacy; from the pitiful soprano notes of such dubious creatures as Marlowe, Jonson, Chapman, Gray, Coleridge, Shelley, Landor, "cum semiviro comitatu," we avert our ears to catch the higher and manlier harmonies of a poet with all his natural parts and powers complete. For truly, if love or knowledge of ancient art and wisdom be the sure mark of "emasculation," and the absence of any taint of such love or any tincture of such knowledge (as then in consistency it must be) the supreme sign of perfect manhood, Mr. Robert Buchanan should be amply competent to renew the thirteenth labour of Hercules.

> "One would not be a young maid in his way
> For more than blushing comes to."

Nevertheless, in a country where (as Mr. Carlyle says in his essay on Diderot) indecent exposure is an offence cognizable at police-offices, it might have been as well for him to uncover with less immodest publicity the gigantic nakedness of his ignorance. Any sense of shame must probably be as alien to the Heracleidan blood as any sense of fear; but the spectators of such an exhibition may be excused if they could wish that at least the shirt of Nessus or another were happily at hand to fling over the more than human display of that massive and muscular impudence, in all the abnormal development of its monstrous proportions. It is possible that our Scottish demigod of song has made too long a sojourn in "the land of Lorne," and learnt from his Highland comrades to dispense in public with what is not usually discarded in any British latitude far south of "the western Hebrides."

At this point, and even after this incomparable windfall in the way of entomology, I begin to doubt whether after all I shall ever make any way as a scientific student. The savours, the forms, the sounds, the contortions, of the singular living things which this science commands us to submit to examination, need a stouter stomach to cope with them than mine. No doubt they have their reasons for being; they were probably meant for some momentary action and passion of their own, harmful or harmless; and how can the naturalist suppose that merely by accurate analysis of their phenomena he has gauged the secret of their mysterious existence? It is so hard to see the reason why they should be, that we are compelled to think the reason must be very grave.

And if once we cease to regard such things scientifically, there is assuredly no reason why we should regard them at all. Historically considered, they have no interest whatever; the historian discerns no perceptible variation in their tribe for centuries on centuries. It is only because this age is not unlike other ages that the children of Zoilus whet their teeth against your epic, the children of Rymer against your play; the children —no, not the children; let us at least be accurate —the successors of Fréron and Desfontaines lift up their throats against your worship of women:

"Monsieur Veuillot t'appelle avec esprit citrouille;"

Mr. Buchanan indicates to all Hebridean eyes the flaws and affectations in your style, as in that of an amatory foreigner; Mr. Lowell assures his market that the best coin you have to offer is brass, and more than hints that it is stolen brass—whether from his own or another forehead, he scorns to specify; and the Montrouge Jesuit, the Grubstreet poet, the Mayflower Puritan, finds each his perfect echo in his natural child; in the first voice you catch the twang of Garasse and Nonotte, in the second of Flecknoe and Dennis, in the third of Tribulation Wholesome and Zeal-of-the-Land Busy. Perhaps then after all their use is to show that the age is not a bastard, but the legitimate heir and representative of other centuries; degenerate, if so it please you to say—all ages have been degenerate in their turn—as to its poets and workers, but surely not degenerate as to these. Poor then as it may be in other things, the very lapse of years which has left it weak may help it more surely to determine than stronger ages could the nature of the critical animal. Has not popular opinion passed through wellnigh the same stages with regard to the critic and to the toad? What was thought in the time of Shakespeare by dukes as well as peasants, we may all find written in his verse; but we know now on taking up a Buchanan that, though very ugly, it is not in the least venomous, and assuredly wears no precious jewel in its head. Yet is it rather like a newt or blind-worm than a toad; there is a mendacious air of the old serpent about it at first sight; and the thing is not even viperous: its sting is as false as its tongue is; its very venom is a lie. But when once we have seen the fang, though innocuous, protrude from a mouth which would fain distil poison and can only distil froth, we need no revelation to assure us that the doom of the creature is to go upon its belly and eat dust all the days of its life.

THE END.

ERRATA.

Page 32, last line but one—*for* monsieurs, *read* messieurs.
,, 61, line 19—*for* Πολλὸς, *read* Πολὺς.
,, 72, line 18—*for* Hugos, *read* Hugo's.
,, ,, line 19—*for* Brownings, *read* Browning's.

Titles in This Series

Criticism: General, Poetic, and Dramatic

1. Alfred Austin. THE POETRY OF THE PERIOD. 1870

2. Robert Buchanan. A LOOK ROUND LITERATURE. 1887

3. John William Cole. THE LIFE AND THEATRICAL TIMES OF CHARLES KEAN, F.S.A. 1859. (In two volumes)

4. E. S. Dallas. POETICS: AN ESSAY ON POETRY. 1852

5. E. S. Dallas. THE GAY SCIENCE. 1866

6. H. Buxton Forman. OUR LIVING POETS: AN ESSAY IN CRITICISM. 1871

7. Walter Hamilton. THE AESTHETIC MOVEMENT IN ENGLAND, third edition, 1882

8. R. H. Horne, editor. A NEW SPIRIT OF THE AGE, second edition. 1844. (In two volumes)

9. Madge Kendall. THE DRAMA. 1884. with DRAMATIC OPINIONS. 1890

10. Joseph A. Knight. A HISTORY OF THE STAGE DURING THE VICTORIAN ERA. 1901

11. Lord William Pitt Lennox. PLAYS, PLAYERS, AND PLAYHOUSES AT HOME AND ABROAD. 1881.
(In two volumes)

12. Robert James Mann. TENNYSON'S "MAUD" VINDICATED: AN EXPLANATORY ESSAY. 1856

13. Mowbray Morris. ESSAYS IN THEATRICAL CRITICISM. 1882

14. Henry Neville. THE STAGE: ITS PAST AND PRESENT IN RELATION TO FINE ART. 1875

15. "Q" [Thomas Purnell]. DRAMATISTS OF THE PRESENT DAY. 1871

16. Walter Raleigh. STYLE. 1897

17. William Caldwell Roscoe. POEMS AND ESSAYS (volume two, ESSAYS, only). 1860

18. Clement Scott. THE DRAMA OF YESTERDAY & TODAY. 1899. (In two volumes)

19. James Field Stanfield. AN ESSAY ON THE STUDY AND COMPOSITION OF BIOGRAPHY. 1813

Parody, Satire, Literary Controversy, and Curiosa

20. Edward Bulwer-Lytton. THE NEW TIMON. 1846.

with Algernon Charles Swinburne. SPECIMENS OF MODERN POETS. THE HEPTALOGIA, OR THE SEVEN AGAINST SENSE. 1880. with Algernon Charles Swinburne. "DISGUST: A DRAMATIC MONOLOGUE." 1898

21. [William E. Aytoun and Theodore Martin.] THE BOOK OF BALLADS: EDITED BY BON GAULTIER. 1845. with [William E. Aytoun.] FERMILIAN: OR THE STUDENT OF BADAJOZ: A SPASMODIC TRAGEDY BY T. PERCY JONES. 1854

22. James Carnegie. JONAS FISHER: A POEM IN BROWN AND WHITE. 1875. with [A. C. Swinburne.] THE DEVIL'S DUE: A LETTER TO THE EDITOR OF "THE EXAMINER." BY THOMAS MAITLAND. 1875

23. Philip James Bailey. THE AGE; A COLLOQUIAL SATIRE. 1858

24. [W. C. Bennett.] ANTI-MAUD. 1856. with [Eustace Clare Grenville Murray.] THE COMING K———. 1873. with [W. H. Mallock.] EVERY MAN HIS OWN POET. 1877

25. [John Burley Waring.] POEMS INSPIRED BY CERTAIN PICTURES AT THE ART TREASURES EXHIBITION, MANCHESTER. 1857. with [Anon.] THE LAUGHTER OF THE MUSES. 1869

26. Robert Buchanan. THE FLESHLY SCHOOL OF POETRY AND OTHER PHENOMENA OF THE DAY. 1872.

with Algernon Charles Swinburne. UNDER THE MICROSCOPE. 1872

27. J. Rutter. THE NINETEENTH CENTURY, A POEM, IN TWENTY-NINE CANTOS. 1900

Collections of Critical Essays

28. William E. Fredeman, editor. VICTORIAN PREFACES AND INTRODUCTIONS: A FACSIMILE COLLECTION. 1986

29. Ira Bruce Nadel, editor. VICTORIAN FICTION: A COLLECTION OF ESSAYS FROM THE PERIOD. 1986

30. Ira Bruce Nadel, editor. VICTORIAN BIOGRAPHY: A COLLECTION OF ESSAYS FROM THE PERIOD. 1986

31. John F. Stasny, editor. VICTORIAN POETRY: A COLLECTION OF ESSAYS FROM THE PERIOD. 1986

32. William E. Fredeman, editor. THE VICTORIAN POETS: AN ALPHABETICAL COMPILATION OF THE BIO-CRITICAL INTRODUCTIONS TO THE VICTORIAN POETS FROM A. H. MILES'S "THE POETS AND POETRY OF THE NINETEENTH CENTURY." 1986

LIBRARY OF DA